The Political Limits of
Environmental Regulation

Recent Titles from Quorum Books

The Employment Contract: Rights and Duties of Employers and Employees
Warren Freedman

Lobbying and Government Relations: A Guide for Executives
Charles S. Mack

U.S. Protectionism and the World Debt Crisis
Edward John Ray

The Social and Economic Consequences of Deregulation: The Transportation Industry in Transition
Paul Stephen Dempsey

The Accountant's Guide to Corporation, Partnership, and Agency Law
Sidney M. Wolf

Human Information Processing in Accounting
Ahmed Belkaoui

Alternative Transportation Fuels
Daniel Sperling

The Design and Implementation of Administrative Controls: A Guide for Financial Executives
John P. Fertakis

Financial Futures and Options: A Guide to Markets, Applications, and Strategies
Todd E. Petzel

Problem Employees and Their Personalities: A Guide to Behaviors, Dynamics, and Intervention Strategies for Personnel Specialists
William T. Martin

The Banking System in Troubled Times: New Issues of Stability and Continuity
Jeremy F. Taylor

Real Interest Rates and Investment Borrowing Strategy
Peter S. Spiro

THE POLITICAL LIMITS OF ENVIRONMENTAL REGULATION

Tracking the Unicorn

BRUCE YANDLE

Quorum Books
New York • Westport, Connecticut • London

Library of Congress Cataloging-in-Publication Data

Yandle, Bruce.
   The political limits of environmental regulation : tracking the
unicorn / Bruce Yandle.
      p.   cm.
   Bibliography: p.
   Includes index.
   ISBN 0-89930-431-1 (lib. bdg. : alk. paper)
   1. Environmental policy—United States.   2. Environmental
protection—United States.   I. Title.
HC110.E5Y36   1989
363.7'056'0973—dc20   89–32919

British Library Cataloguing in Publication Data is available.

Library of Congress Catalog Card Number: 89–32919
ISBN: 0-89930-431-1

First published in 1989 by Quorum Books

Greenwood Press, Inc.
88 Post Road West, Westport, Connecticut   06881

Printed in the United States of America

∞™

The paper used in this book complies with the
Permanent Paper Standard issued by the National
Information Standards Organization (Z39.48–1984).

10 9 8 7 6 5 4 3 2 1

Contents

Tables

Preface

This book is about political economy and the application of economic logic to politics. It focuses on America's effort to regulate environmental quality, a saga that is now some twenty years old. In a very real sense, writing the book has provided an opportunity to place between two covers gleanings from my professional career as a teacher, researcher, government economist, and consultant. Much of that work has involved government regulation and, within that broad subject, regulation of the environment.

My attempt to provide the reader with a detailed story about the political limits of environmental regulation reflects the development of my thinking about the problem of federal regulation. In the 1970s, I was primarily an efficiency seeker, believing that good lessons in basic economics properly presented would sharply limit the number of federal regulations that seemed to cost so much but yield so little in the way of net social benefits.

After some experience working in Washington, I learned that economic ignorance was not the source of the problem. Indeed, the level of economic understanding among career bureaucrats, politicians, and their appointees was quite high. The problem of efficiency and any apparent lack of it related to the interplay of politics, economics, and the institutions that order our lives. Before mounting an efficiency charger, I decided it would make sense first to understand the workings of the institutions being challenged. That, I discovered, was a tall order.

By now enough books have been written on environmental

law and policy, benefit-cost analysis of environmental regulation, and efficiency analysis of the Environmental Protection
Agency (EPA) to fill a long library shelf. But as yet, no single
book has been written that examines unrelentingly the political economy of environmental control.

The emphasis and analysis found throughout this book reflect major episodes in my professional life and work. In 1969,
while a graduate student at Georgia State University, I began working earnestly to understand the evolution of property
rights and markets. That led to a dissertation that focused on
externalities—spillover effects—in housing markets and how
urban blight, a popular term at the time, might be recognized
and dealt with.

On coming to Clemson University in the fall of 1969, I became involved in research on water pollution and the management of water quality. That research has resulted in a number
of research reports, two books, and a number of articles in professional journals, and it continues.

In 1976–77, I worked in Washington as a Senior Economist
on the President's Council on Wage and Price Stability, where
I was responsible for reviewing all newly proposed major regulations from the Environmental Protection Agency. That work
involved evaluating the cost-effectiveness of the many proposed rules, with an eye toward increasing their net benefits
while preserving beneficial market forces as much as possible.

It was during that stay that I became involved in the primi-
tive development of EPA's offset and bubble concepts, ideas
that related to my dissertation work on property rights to environmental assets. I also filled my head with details on major
EPA legislation and rules. From that time forward, I followed
the evolution of EPA rules and actions.

Returning to Washington and the Council on Wage and Price
Stability in the summer of 1978, I continued my analysis of
environmental regulations by studying the new 1977 amendments to the nation's basic water and air pollution laws. Then
in 1982–84, I worked as Executive Director of the Federal
Trade Commission, where I was also responsible for the agency's regulatory intervention program, an activity that involved
preparing analyses and testimony for regulatory proceedings

at other agencies. I was again involved in work on the evolution of environmental regulation.

The "public choice" focus found throughout the book emphasizes explanation, not condemnation. With regard to the environmental saga, the approach seeks to explain why cost-effectiveness and efficiency count for little in U.S. regulatory policy; why little attention is paid to outcomes, but much is devoted to political process; why in addition to failing to focus on a report card of progress, those who seek more environmental regulation often aid and assist the very industry that is scorned; and why we should not expect to see much in the way of regulatory reform that could clearly bring more environmental quality at much lower cost.

The realization that seeking an understanding of why the world works the way it does, as opposed to working simply to change the world, marked the beginning of a major inquiry into the political economy of regulation. From that point on, my work emphasized empirical investigations that sought to identify the chief elements of major and sometimes minor regulatory episodes. Of course, there were still times when I put on an efficiency seeker's hat and argued for particular policies and stronger economic analysis of them.

While the book attempts to capture and report my work on environmental regulation, along with that of my students, it also provides summaries of major works by many important scholars who have contributed mightily to the same kind of inquiry. For that reason, I hope the detailed references and footnotes will be valuable to other scholars in the field.

I hope the book will appeal to a large audience of readers. (What else might an author say?) Those who teach college courses in government regulation, policy studies, and administrative law should find it useful to their students. Others in the environmental community, including active workers in environmental organizations, lobbyists, members of congressional staffs, and business managers who occasionally work the halls of Washington will find some familiar stories here, as well as some new interpretations of them.

While I hope that many readers will find the book rewarding, I also recognize that many may be disturbed, if not angered, by it. Efforts to explain the way the world works seldom paint flattering pictures of those who actually struggle in the process. There are instances where all parties to the environmental saga will likely take offense at my interpretations, though that is certainly not my intention. In that sense, the treatment of the subject can be called even-handed.

Since the research and writing reflected here encompasses so many years of my work and therefore so many instances of insight and assistance provided by colleagues, former teachers, students, and critics, I will refrain from attempting to list that large number of names. Instead, I shall express a debt of deep gratitude to and register my profound respect for Hugh H. Macaulay, my colleague and occasional coauthor, who has provided me with years of inspiration and education. The extent to which the book generates more light than heat reflects lessons learned from Hugh's stalwart effort always to get the story straight. I also offer gladly my appreciation to my wife, Dot, for having read and improved the manuscript with her graceful attention to logic and style.

In a broader and more general sense, I express appreciation to Clemson University for providing a hospitable atmosphere for twenty years of thinking, teaching, and writing, and to those organizations that over the years supported Clemson's environmental research effort in the Department of Economics. Chief among those are the Department of Interior and E.I. DuPont de Nemours.

The Political Limits of
Environmental Regulation

1

The U.S. Environmental Saga: How It Began

INTRODUCTION

This book is about political limits to environmental control. It is not a polemic about the usefulness of economic incentives for minimizing the cost of controlling pollution, though failed attempts to implement such strategies are discussed and some polemical statements may creep in here and there. Nor is the book about the significant deterioration of America's biological heritage and how little progress seems to be made in mitigating the damages of pollution, though that too is discussed, sometimes extensively.

Instead, this book attempts to describe elements of America's struggle to control environmental quality in ways that explain why economically efficient controls are seldom, if ever, adopted and why so little progress is made in achieving environmental goals.

In that sense, the book is about a unicorn—something that seems very real and logical, yet is unattainable. Achievement of such things as zero pollution is a political unicorn, as is the notion that things might be done at lowest possible cost. An understanding of the political economy of federal environmental regulation illustrates why unicorns are politically valuable, and why the lofty goals of environmental quality will always be unicorns.

This chapter sets the tone for the book by describing ways of considering America's environmental saga, the evolution of the problem and solutions to it, and interest group stories that compete to explain what has happened.

BACKGROUND TO THE ENVIRONMENTAL SAGA

In the late 1960s, when America was riding the crest of an economy juiced up by inflation, many cries and whispers were raised across the land. The population was young, and the idealism of youth found its way into many public policies. There was an appeal for purity, for perfection. We Americans seemed to think government could reorder our world to provide unlimited simultaneous benefits. We ordered safer cars and highways, flawless toys, foods, and drugs. And we instructed the federal government to provide marked improvements in environmental quality.

The mood of the times was presented by Tom Paxton in the song "Whose Garden Was This?" Reflecting on a lost garden, Paxton made reference to man's stewardship of the heavenly gift and asked about flowers, rivers, clear water, how those things must have looked, and what happened. The behavior of the owner was a central part of the song, suggesting that any reasonable owner would have protected such a lovely garden.

The words of the song cut to the bone of the issue: Whose river was it? There was a fundamental problem with property rights. If property rights could somehow be defined, the solution to pollution would soon be in the offing. But the new property contemplated by the more active environmentalists was not to be private. They demanded a new kind of public property.

Their theme was expressed in song, sermons, sit-ins, teach-ins, and marches to capital buildings. Earth Day, bumper stickers, and T-shirts called for a new ethic.

In public sector efforts to clean up, industrial plants were turned away from seashores, reflecting public preference for tourism, which sometimes generated more pollution than the spurned industry might have done. But tourism looked cleaner. Our love for purity brought demands for legislation, an environmental ethic with a legal mandate. The nation set out to clean up water, land, and sky. Dilution as the solution to pollution was dead.

Twenty years have passed since the outset of the environmental revolution, one of modern history's major social episodes. Coming of age in the late 1960s, the environmental movement generated political responses much like those of the Granger and Progressive movements a century earlier. In the earlier period, Supreme Court decisions extended the reach of the state to regulate prices and other economic relationships and said, "Property does become clothed with a public interest when used in a manner to make it of public consequence, and affect the community at large."[1] Federal regulation followed soon after that decision, and the Interstate Commerce Commission, organized in 1887, set in motion the beginning of all-encompassing regulation in the United States.

The public interest arguments of the nineteenth century formed an important part of the underlying logic for the 1955 Air Pollution Control Act, the Water Pollution Control Act Amendments of 1956, the Water Quality Act of 1965, the Clean Air Act of 1963, and the Motor Vehicle Air Pollution Control Act of 1965.[2] These legislative actions revised rules of property and defined new property. They laid the foundation for extensive federal actions that reached far beyond control of the natural environment.

The high-pitched public argument put forward by some environmentalists in the 1970s was so convincing that private property and capitalism as an economic process became suspect. Before the environmental revolution, many had lauded the uplifting qualities of the market and the incentives it provided its participants to consider all costs in their decision making, including environmental ones. That was forgotten, or at least overshadowed, in the 1970s. New voices spoke out about external effects, spillovers, and the apparent inability of the market to handle the disposal of wastes, the riskiness of drugs and chemicals, and the elimination of hazards that somehow seemed destined to destroy the foundations of modern life.

Government control was viewed optimistically as more nearly approaching perfection than the much decried market mechanism. A federal environmental control saga began, one that continues to this day. Since then, serious questions have been raised as to which mechanism—the unfettered market, state and local rules, or federal regulation—might be most likely to fail when dealing with environmental use.

Are There Evolutionary Phases?

Although man's welfare was clearly a concern in the early stages of the environmental movement, as seen in the definition of primary air quality standards that related to human health and welfare, other worries about plants, trees, water, and other life-forms were raised to an equally important level. Looking back with less emotional eyes, let us attempt to discern certain phases in the process that appear to reflect progress toward a rational destination. Our starting point must be one of totally unrestricted use of the environment.

In the first phase, all the natural environment was a common-access resource. It simply must be that way. Before the advent of property rights and restrictive rules, natural resources are like manna from heaven. The endowment is so large that all who wish to consume have enough. When the earthly commons become crowded, people move at low cost to a more favorable environment. In a somewhat modern setting, it is a story about steel mills discharging waste to rivers that flow with such volume that dilution solves the pollution problem.

The second phase begins with environmental scarcity. With population growth and continued expansion of demand for the production of goods, greater use of the environment and limited alternatives to it generate economic scarcity. In the absence of rules to allocate the common-access resource, too much degradation occurs. Pollution becomes a real problem, one that imposes more costs than benefits. It is a story of typhoid epidemics, damaged populations of aquatic life and forests, a story about efforts to regain control of environmental use.

Enter the age of holy water. This evolutionary phase can include a community movement that focuses first on the nature of the pollution threat and then struggles to limit man's encroachment on the threatened environment. There is an attempt to gain time to research the problem and devise new controls. Major rules arrive that understandably embody a hands-off logic and set unrealistic, but much appreciated, goals for achieving dramatic reductions in waste discharge.

The lofty legislation that ensues gradually becomes translated into more detailed regulations. What in some ways corresponded to a holy war against pollution is transformed to a multigoal bureaucratic endeavor that produces extensive rules of behavior for the goods-producing economy. Those who resist the movement while stubbornly arguing about benefits, costs, international competitiveness, and the regulatory burden to be borne by people are generally viewed with the courtesy reserved for Neanderthal men. Those favoring strict controls argue that no matter how large the yet unknown costs might prove to be, the goal to be accomplished would be worth the price. After all, the problem is seen as being life threatening. Mankind's common garden must be cleansed.

The third phase of the evolution of new environmental property finds the public sector guardian doing its work. It is a period of public property. Rules are in place, the environment is rationed, and realism begins to replace romanticism. Through limited experimentation, the public sector managers search for pragmatic approaches that offer the promise of cost-effective control. With the arrival of public property managers, an age of economic environment emerges and displaces the earlier phases of common access and holy water.

Emerging markets for environmental resources mark the end of the evolutionary story. Continued management of environmental use imparts learning about polluting activities, the competing demand for environmental quality, the relative costs and benefits of different control strategies, and how to monitor and ration environmental use. That learning contributes to a process that clothes certain features of the environment with tradeable property rights. The features of the environment that can be traded then join aspects of land-use that entered the market centuries before. Markets for environmental property rights evolve, and part of the problem of conflicting use is resolved.

The evolutionary phases described here are tied to the evolution of property rights and markets. Somewhat paradoxically, institutions at first condemned for their failings reemerge as devices for resolving the problem. Common-access resources become private property. Inefficiency and waste become efficiency and productivity. Scarcity is the prelude to plenty.

The evolution of federal management of the environment contains some of these phases. By the late 1970s, federal regulation of certain features of the environment and other risky aspects of life was an accepted fact, though each and every feature of regulation, new and old, was subject to controversy and contest. With the implementation of the many rules, the formerly hypothetical costs became real, and the ultimate question could be raised in respectable discourse: How clean is clean enough?

About the same time, concern about toxic substances and the ultimate disposal of waste began to overshadow the conceptually simpler yet unachievable goal of reducing pollution to zero. Some features of the environment entered an economic age, where benefits and costs could at least be discussed. Newer features of the problem entered an age of holy water. The process repeated.

In the 1980s, attention became focused on risk assessment and risk management, the first presented as inherently scientific, the other as political. In some ways, the new emphasis brought memories of the 1970s. Instead of zero pollution, the new direction called for zero risk.

Examination of the environmental saga leaves an indelible impression that there are regular cycles of reaction and action as America grapples with a series of apparent environmental threats. Along with the cycles came the knowledge that arguably illuminated some dimensions of the next problem. Social learning became embodied in the arcane pages of each package of legislation and the Federal Register. First the people, then their political agents, the legislature, and finally the agents of the legislators worked to solve each problem as it surfaced and threatened society.

The Evolving Flagship Agency

The U.S. Environmental Protection Agency emerged in 1970 as a political response to the search for ways to regulate environmental use. In a way, the agency was full grown at birth with 5,700 workers at the agency and an operating budget of $1 billion in its first year.[3] It was full grown mainly because it was not really new. It was a conglomeration of pieces of older agencies that carried with them a concentration of statutes to be administered by the new entity.

By 1974, a year when massive expenditures were made for construction of municipal treatment plants, the agency had 9,100 workers and a budget of $8.3 billion. Ten years later, in 1984, the agency had 11,400 workers. Now a mature agency with even more items of legislation to enforce, EPA in 1988 had approximately 14,500 workers and expected to add 1,000 more in 1989.

Across the years 1970–1987, the agency experienced a compounded employment growth rate of 5 percent, while real GNP grew at a rate of 2.7 percent. However, much of the growth occurred before 1980, when it might be argued that the agency was catching up with its task and the economy. Social learning was arguably taking place. Since that year, the ranks of the agency have grown at an annual rate of 3.3 percent, much closer to the economy's growth rate of about 2.9 percent.

EPA's relative political importance is seen when its growth rate is compared with other agencies that also responded to the holy water mandate of the late 1960s.[4] The Food and Drug Administration's ranks grew from 4,414 in 1970 to 6,834 in 1987, a growth rate of 2.5 percent. The Consumer Product Safe-

Table 1
**Index Reflecting the Proportion of the *New York Times* Space
Devoted to Stories Dealing with Environmental Pollution**

Year	Water Pollution	Air Pollution	Solid Waste
1954	0.26	0.54	0.24
1956	0.17	0.35	0.74
1958	0.48	0.48	0.42
1960	0.44	0.59	0.14
1962	0.70	0.47	0.10
1964	1.05	0.56	0.09
1966	1.42	1.42	0.25
1968	1.36	1.17	1.94
1970	7.60	5.55	1.64
1972	4.83	3.38	1.56
1974	2.91	2.59	1.76
1976	4.55	2.50	1.40
1978	2.28	1.39	1.72
1980	2.54	1.97	1.52
1982	2.25	1.63	4.09
1984	1.85	0.97	3.94
1986	1.57	1.49	3.06

Note: The index is formed by multiplying the share of total pages in the *New York Times Index* accounted for by each pollution category by 1000. Data for the years 1954–1974 are from Hugh H. Macaulay and Bruce Yandle, *Environmental Use and the Market*, Lexington, Mass.: Lexington Books, 1977, p. 2. Data for remaining years are calculated from the *Index*.

ty Commission had 884 employees in 1975, its peak year, and entered 1987 with 456 workers. The National Highway Safety Administration's work force rose from 518 in 1970 to 640 in 1987. Outstripping the EPA record, the Nuclear Regulatory Commission saw its 1970 work force of 688 rise to 3,218 in 1987 to yield a growth rate of 9 percent.

The EPA's growth reflects environmental legislation passed by Congress since the heyday of the late 1960s when concern about pollution created a groundswell of popular support for government action. The newspaper space devoted to various aspects of the environment is just one indicator of the rising tide of interest that emerged for various categories of pollution.

Table 1 contains indexes by year for pollution-related stories in the *New York Times* from 1954 through 1986. As seen in the table, there was early and growing interest in water and air pollution, which peaked in 1970 and generally declined thereafter. Interest in solid waste management, as reflected in the index, rose from rather low levels in the 1960s, peaked in 1982, and continues at a relatively high level. The cycles of action and reaction mentioned previously are mirrored in the pages of the nation's leading daily newspaper.

The Legislation

Major pieces of national legislation followed the demand for political action reflected in the news stories indexes. Meaningful water pollution control legislation in 1967 was followed in 1972 by the Federal Water Pollution Control Act, which established the fundamental blueprint still being followed. Important air pollution legislation came in 1970, and other significant acts dealing with more specific pollutants such as solid waste, noise, pesticides, and hazardous waste came later.

The Conservation Foundation has logically divided the major legislation that underlies EPA's operations into two categories, which again reflect a cyclical process.[5] The Foundation refers to statutes that focus on "conventional pollutants" and those that deal with toxic substances. The dichotomy somehow suggests there are well-established smoothly operating procedures for dealing with the conventional pollutants, that they are in an advanced part of the evolutionary cycle, but that things are still to be worked out for the others. Table 2 lists the current stock of EPA-managed legislation and the year each law was passed.

Closer examination of the data on EPA's growth and the corresponding legislation again suggests that environmental hazards have been assigned priorities and that the machinery of government is working to generate solutions to the problems.

Table 2
Federal Environmental Legislation by Type of Pollutant

Conventional Pollutants

1970 Clean Air Act
1970 Resource Recovery Act
1972 Federal Water Pollution Control Act
1972 Noise Control Act
1976 Noise Act Amendments

Toxic Pollutants

1972 Federal Environmental Pesticide
     Control Act
1974 Safe Drinking Water Act
1974 Resource Conservation and Recovery
     Act (RCRA)
1976 Toxic Substances Control Act
1977 Clean Air Act Amendments
1977 Clean Water Act
1978 Federal Insecticide, Fungicide and
     Rodenticide Act Amendments
1980 Comprehensive Environmental Response
     Compensation and Liability Act
     (Superfund)
1984 Hazardous and Solid Waste Amendments
     to RCRA
1986 Superfund Amendments and Reauthorization
     Act

COMPETING VISIONS

It may be mentally stimulating and perhaps comforting to search for and find a rational explanation for America's troubled search for ways to manage environmental quality, but attempting to do so may be stretching things beyond the realm of reason. The notion of evolving property rights is probably sound, but it is unreasonable to think that property rights to all the surface water and the air mantle that covers the entire United States would somehow surface simultaneously, all in the early 1970s.

The development process simply doesn't work that way. Property rights have historically emerged slowly on a piece-meal basis, and the enforcement of those rights usually rests at the community level. It is simply unbelievable that commonly held community values, the stuff that forms and protects property, could be reflected in uniform laws written for an area as vast and diverse as the United States. As we shall see, that is a central part of the problem that sets limits on the political protection of environmental quality.

Thinking about broad social cycles that generate efficient outcomes and hoping that something as heterogeneous as water and air quality could be controlled homogeneously is logically appealing but fails to reflect the reality of the problem being addressed. Since the beginning of federal regulation in the United States, one ideological camp has believed that publicly interested experts could be assembled in Washington to find scientifically and economically sound solutions to pressing social problems.

Those holding that view optimistically see the social system as something that can be managed in ways that agree with their view of a good society. They hold to the notion that federally written rules can somehow protect individuals, firms, and other organizations from their own worst tendencies.

The phases of the environmental saga described earlier suggest that we pass through the regulatory phase when logical expertise applies command-and-control solutions to the problem of environmental decay. Private property rights and economic incentives that cause people to behave in socially beneficial ways become the terminal station in the evolutionary trip.

Unfortunately, that outcome is completely at odds with the mechanism expected to generate the property rights result. Those who favor scientifically determined command and control regulation generally do not support the use of incentives that rely on unbridled individual choice in matters environmental. The property rights school and the regulation school are populated by people who think differently. They are naturally at odds with each other.

The underlying differences in the two ways of addressing environmental and other social problems are described indirectly and extensively by two very different writers. Economist Thomas Sowell in his book, *A Conflict of Visions*, focuses directly on the problem.[6] He places people in two polarized camps. Those in the first camp have an unconstrained view of man and believe accordingly that properly chosen knowledgeable people can find and impose regulatory solutions to social problems. The second camp is populated by people who have a constrained vision of man, believing that social systems evolve in complex ways that provide incentives for fallible people to achieve socially useful results, even when the social end is no part of the people's intentions.

Applying these incompatible visions to environmental control suggests that command-and-control regulation satisfies the unconstrained view of man. The evolution of property rights and markets where efficient environmental use is not directed but occurs spontaneously through uncoordinated group action satisfies the constrained view. As Sowell points out in his extensive discussion of the conflict, we should not expect one approach to emerge from the other.

Another view of conflicting visions to be applied here is developed by the late philosopher-author, Robert Pirsig, in his fascinating book, *Zen and the Art of Motorcycle Maintenance*.[7] Like Sowell, Pirsig divides mankind into two camps, those who hold to a romantic view of the world and others who have a classical understanding. In terms of the title of his book, the romantics enjoy the thrill of nature that comes with motorcycle riding. The others welcome that thrill but link it to an appreciation of the machine and the interconnected parts that deliver the experience. The second group is keenly aware of linkages and systems and see the world as "underlying form itself."

The romantics, chiefly interested in immediate appearances, seek environmental quality for its own sake, perhaps believing that rules can be designed and imposed to generate desired outcomes immediately. Their vision of human agents who might engage in strategic behavior when confronting the rules contains such unfortunate behavior as stemming from ignorance and immorality, things that have to be dealt with by more enlightened social servants.

Those who see the world as built from complex intertwined relationships that reflect competing human values scoff at the idea of command and control, arguing that one cannot simply alter one part of the system without disturbing its entire mechanism. Unlike ecologists who have a supreme appreciation of the complex linkages that generate any natural life system, but who generally fail to include man's response to economic incentives in that system, those holding the classical view of the environment include man in all his manifestations in the ecological system.

Those holding to the constrained view believe the market system is a reflection of the world's underlying form. Prices evolve from the systems of property rights and contracts. Property right owners bear the costs of their errors and receive rewards from other members of society when resources are managed efficiently. Price signals encourage all market participants to economize. Indeed, none can use a property-protected resource unless voluntary agreement is reached with the owners. Clothing elements of the environment in property rights fits the resource into the market system. But taking that step does not automatically ensure a preconceived outcome.

The romantic, like the person with the unconstrained view, is impatient with all this and can hardly be expected to accept an uncontrolled outcome for things as important to him as air and water quality. So we have a conflict. One group focuses on social processes that can lead to improved results. Attempting to control the process spoils its overall effectiveness. The other group focuses on specific problems—sulfur dioxide emissions, hazardous wastes—rather than on processes, and seeks to alter outcomes by directing human action.

Competing visions are reflected in political competition that is often described by two very different stories about what might be expected when politicians and their appointees seek to solve environmental problems.

Two Competing Stories

The earlier paragraphs in this chapter outline one story about the environmental saga, a struggle to bring overall improvement to America's market economy, a story about regulatory approaches designed ostensibly to internalize external costs, improve environmental quality, and maximize human welfare at minimum cost. It is a public interest story of muddling toward efficiency. It is a story of frustration, mistakes, dealing with one form of pollution and then another, but nonetheless of progress toward an efficient outcome. In that sense, it is an optimistic story.

The competing vision discussion suggests there is another story, one that contains some of the same public interest motivations, but one that allows for special interest groups operating in a representative democracy to tilt the political steering wheel and guide legislators as they devise the rules and regulations. That story contains the same stages, an apparent evolution of property rights, and arguments about efficiency. But unlike the first, the second story concludes that the environmental saga became a struggle about territories, protected groups, raising competitors' costs, a story more about frustration than progress toward achieving economic and environmental goals.

These two competing stories relate directly to ideas about competing visions, but not quite in the way Sowell explains the situation. Yes, there is conflict between camps who wish to change things for the better. But there is also an odd kind of cooperation. The cooperation is not direct. Indeed, it is most likely uncoordinated. Instead, the camp that calls for government direction of the economy as the appropriate way to solve environmental problems provides the rationale needed by others who simply want less competition.

Of course, there are totally different social visions that underlie the two competing stories. The first views government as being removed from the social forces that play through a separate private sector. On the one hand, people urge their preferences on politicians through the voting mechanism where each citizen has one vote. On the other, self interest and dollars drive the process. This vision sees government as a corrective force that balances a people's baser desires for goods and wealth against their collective desires for commonly sought improvements to be shared by all.

The second story about strange coalitions emphasizes one world in which political and economic forces play. Other than in some academic's mind, there are no separate private and public sectors. There are just people and organizations of people who strive to better themselves. This vision sees voting and buying goods as market processes since voters can be influenced with tax dollar benefits and politicians can be influenced with campaign contributions.

Public interest arguments are crucially important in both worlds. In the first case, the political mechanism reflects nothing but the public interest. Social efficiency is the ultimate goal, and that is where environmental regulation will take us. In the second, political actions that might serve private interests must always be clothed with the public interest. Some public interest benefits will be generated, since that is necessary for private interests to be served.

Both stories deserve our attention since the evidence suggests both have something to offer. Each episode of the environmental saga we will examine, whether it be for controlling water and air pollution or for regulating the final disposal of hazardous waste, has been accompanied by passionate rhetoric about environmental degradation, risks, and pending catastrophes. The public interest arguments will always be present. Responding to public opinion molded by the rhetoric, each regulatory episode has begun with goals that are both technically and economically impossible to achieve. But of course, it is in the nature of political language to hold up high promises of social achievement. Sadly, however, the environmental legislation goes beyond even that.

The machinery invented by Congress for dealing with each category of pollution has been flawed so that efficient control cannot be accomplished. Actual progress never meets the promise of the legislation, and actual costs are inevitably larger than those originally estimated. But oddly enough, the pattern repeats for each new effort to control another dimension of the environment, as if no one ever learns about failed promises, or no one really cares.

The regular appearance of these characteristics—unmet promises and escalated costs—supports either of two hypotheses. The first argues that Congress is indeed motivated to serve the public interest but systematically makes mistakes, always overestimates economic realities, never learns from the past, and is incapable of developing legislation to accomplish the public interest goals it seeks to achieve.

In sharp contrast, the competing hypothesis says that no group of intelligent legislators will systematically make such mistakes, certainly not for twenty years running. That hypothesis argues instead that Congress understands what it is doing but deliberately does not seek efficient solutions to environmental problems. It tells us that Congress serves many competing interests when developing environmental legislation, and that environmental symbols are often more important in these struggles than substance.

It is fundamentally important to understand the way the world works, to find logical explanations of the outcomes that emerge from politically important struggles. That is why this book directly examines the political limits of environmental regulation and focuses on the regulatory institutions, the motivations of the major actors involved in the struggles, and the outcomes that derive from those actions.

This book is organized to address these important considerations. It necessarily focuses on the U.S. Environmental Protection Agency (EPA) and several major actions taken by the lead agency in America's federal struggle to regulate environmental use. But while that focus is necessary, it is also misleading. The EPA and all other agents of Congress respond to their principal, which is Congress. So what might be taken as either praise or criticism of EPA should rightfully be interpreted as comments about Congress and that body's efforts to balance interest group demand for government action.

The book does not pretend to cover all of the major regulatory episodes having to do with environmental quality since 1970. But it does focus on some of the major ones and also examines pre-federal environmental regulation and the social forces that partly explain the evolution of federal regulation. Major attention is devoted to the federal air pollution story, since much of my research has been on that topic. But even there little is said about the control of pollution from automobiles and other mobile sources. There are chapters that include discussions of the water pollution control story, toxic wastes and Superfund, and the economic and environmental effects of the EPA saga.

But before embarking on the story itself, it is necessary to develop a theoretical framework that underlies the telling of it. The next chapter of the book does that by examining a theory I call Bootleggers and Baptists. It takes a closer look at the odd political coalitions that almost inevitably appear when federal regulation is developed. Unlike the remaining chapters in the book, this one does not focus solely on environmental regulation. Instead, the chapter examines a number of diverse regulatory episodes, which suggests that the logic of the argument developed there is robust and capable of being generalized.

Chapter 3 describes how environmental regulation developed in the United States long before the involvement of the federal government. Beginning with early common law cases dealing with nuisance and trespass, the chapter carries the story forward describing early local ordinances, county regulations, state laws, and then multistate compacts. The chapter paints a picture of evolving controls, flexibility, and variety.

Chapter 4 outlines the rise and development of federal regulation, including the early struggles that had to do with flexibility versus uniformity. Ultimately, uniform command and control regulation win out, and the nation becomes involved in a continental effort to achieve the newly set national standards. Controversies and disappointments enter the story, and opposing special interest groups appear regularly in the episodes recounted.

Having described much of the federal saga in Chapter 4, the next chapter discusses the lack of apparent interest in efficient pollution control. Early efforts to use economic incentives are described, yet inefficient command and control always seems to win out in the political economy that surrounds the efficiency seekers.

Chapter 6 addresses a current environmental issue, the control of hazardous waste. Again, background to the problem indicates the arrival of a new crisis, one that must be addressed by federal regulators. The development of Superfund, the incentives included in it, and the disappointments with the program are described. The chapter concludes with thoughts about Superfund, EPA, and ways to deal with the impossible situation faced by the regulators.

Having recounted major episodes in the U.S. environmental saga, providing evidence that not much progress has been made, Chapter 7 discusses the economic impact of the many federal rules and regulations, surveying major studies that focus on that topic. Finally, Chapter 8 concludes the book by reflecting on the stories and evidence and once again emphasizing the political limits of environmental control.

NOTES

1. The quotation is from *Munn v. Ill.* (1877). For discussion, see Leonard W. Weiss and Allyn D. Strickland, *Regulation: A Case Approach*, 2d ed. (New York: MacGraw-Hill Book Company, 1982), 199–223.

2. For a discussion of early statutes, see Allen V. Kneese and Charles L. Schultze, *Pollution, Prices, and Public Policy* (Washington: The Brookings Institution, 1975), 30–50.

3. The data on work years and budgets are in nominal terms and are taken from *Budget of the United States Government* (Washington: Office of Management and Budget, various years).

4. The data on various agency growth rates reported here are based on tables from Melinda Warren and Kenneth Chilton, *1989 Federal Regulatory Budgets and Staffing: Effects of the Reagan Presidency* (St. Louis: Center for the Study of American Business, Washington University, April 1988).

5. See *State of the Environment: An Assessment at Mid-Decade* (Washington: The Conservation Foundation, 1984), 38.

6. Thomas Sowell, *A Conflict of Visions* (New York: William Morrow and Company, 1987).

7. Robert Pirsig, *Zen and the Art of Motorcycle Maintenance* (Toronto: Bantam Books, 1974).

2

Bootleggers, Baptists, and Political Limits

INTRODUCTION

The notion of environmental unicorns and competing visions explored in Chapter 1 sets the mental stage for thinking about the political limits of environmental control. That discussion described Tom Sowell's compelling idea about constrained and unconstrained visions of the world. The unconstrained view looks to strong leadership, moral promptings, and the possibility that human nature can be changed to promote a new environmental ethic. The constrained view argues that man's nature is seldom changed in profound ways. Altering incentives and property right relationships is the most logical way to achieve changes in the way people use the environment.

Since in a democracy all people have access to the political forum, it is only logical that competition develops between groups having different visions and among individuals within groups who have a different agenda for managing the environment. Coalitions form among environmental groups, and competing coalitions are formed among industrial and business groups. Along with these come policy analysts, economists, and others who feel they have something to add to the ongoing debate.

As briefly noted, there are ways that one group can use the arguments of the other to achieve totally different objectives.

Appeals by industrialists to the concerns of environmentalists can generate a political response that improves the position of the petitioning industry while simultaneously and sometimes only figuratively satisfying the environmentalists' interests. At other times, those who have another public interest agenda, such as simply reducing the rate of industrial growth, can use the environmentalists' arguments to achieve that goal by creatively crafting regulations.

This chapter explores how common interests between apparently opposing political groups can lead to special interest benefits.[1] The title implies that groups as different as bootleggers and Baptists often find themselves on the same side of a political argument. Equally strange bedfellows will be found in regulatory conflicts that involve issues as diverse as laws that regulate Sunday retail sales, seat belts, and sulfur dioxide emissions. The chapter offers a theoretical blueprint that forms part of the bedrock for the discussion in later chapters. The diverse array of social regulations are explored. All are rules that limit the actions of individuals, firms, and other organizations, and each case explored underlines the importance of interest group action in the realm of regulation.

IN THE BEGINNING

Regulation of individual behavior by higher authorities is as ancient as the Garden of Eden and as recent as yesterday's *Federal Register*. Adam and Eve chaffed against the ironclad specification standard they confronted, accepted the advice of an independent counselor, engaged in noncompliance activities, and suffered the consequences. They were required to leave a pristine environment where entry was barred and move to a significantly deteriorated competitive location where labor productivity was lower and future regulations would be crafted by their fellow man.

Still today, many people are frustrated by complex environmental rules, seek wise counsel as to how to deal with them, and sometimes pay high penalties when they fail to satisfy the regulator. On the other hand, other people complain about the lack of rules, seek more of them, and lobby fiercely for stricter enforcement.

Yet a third group of people from within the ranks of the frustrated and penalized silently accept regulation and welcome the support of those who seek more of it. Indeed, careful examination of almost any successful regulatory episode suggests that there are winners and losers at the margin, but also that the hats worn by the participants are rarely all black or all white. We understand that regulation, like taxation, redistributes wealth and carries costs. We also know that regulatory reform, like tax reform, alters the former redistribution effects and may relieve some of the burdens of regulation, provided the key parties that originally sought the regulation somehow support the changes.

WHAT THEORY TELLS US

The economic literature on regulation and efforts by special interest groups to gain favors from government—whether they be members of the steel industry or the Sierra Club—illuminates some of the dimensions of the demand for regulation, at least for some of the people in a regulation story. We now understand that some regulated firms view regulation favorably, once they realize government intervention is inevitable. Regulation is not necessarily a government-designed hair shirt that constantly limits the desired actions of these firms. It is more like an old tweed suit that not only fits but also feels good. Indeed, those in the tweed suits get upset when efficiency lovers suggest that the government-imposed suit should be thrown away. They do not want deregulation. Regulation has tilted the economic game in their direction and now protects their position.

Their long-suffering compatriots, itching in their hair shirts, feel differently about the matter, but may not be very successful in a showdown, because they lack the support of another group: Those who seek regulation for reasons that have nothing to do with anticompetitive tweed suits. In other words, there are coalitions that work and others that do not.

The modern theories of regulation that carry us beyond the noble public interest story gain considerable yardage in explaining important aspects of many regulations. A widely cited theory of regulation developed by Richard Posner causes us to focus on transfers of wealth from politically weak to stronger groups.[2] Fundamental work by Nobel Laureate George Stigler and Sam Peltzman ask us to consider special interest groups, to look for differential effects across those groups, and to view regulation as a market process with demanders and suppliers.[3] Stigler and Peltzman also argue that most successful regulation will generate some benefits to consumers, even though the favored producer group will likely gain the most.

Gordon Tullock and Nobel Laureate James Buchanan, founders of the Public Choice school in economics and political science, call our attention to rent-seeking behavior, where government's power to limit competition and output always beckon and where seekers of government favors tend to spend the value of their expected gains while chasing them.[4] Tullock and Buchanan observe regulation as a way to restrict output, raise prices, and foreclose markets to new competition.

Fred McChesney notes that politicians can act as agents in the regulatory game, profiting regardless of the result.[5] He suggests that politicians can propose harsh rules that cause the affected individuals to organize politically and lobby for relief, strengthening the politician's position. Once the rules are in place, the organized group will continue to lobby, supporting those politicians who are sympathetic to their cause.

Economist Gary Becker directs attention to coalitions that favor and oppose actions by government to redistribute wealth, whether that is done by taxing and spending or by wealth-generating regulations that impose a tax to be shared by one and all in the form of deadweight cost to the economy.[6] His analysis focuses on political actions and reactions that are induced when groups seeking governmental favors are countered by others who bear the net cost of those actions.

A NEGLECTED POINT

A host of empirical work now lends strong support to elements of each of these compatible theories. However, while there is room in the new theories for a neglected focus, none of the theories emphasize the potential importance of having public interest support for successful regulatory ventures. It is as though the public interest theory, the pure notion that political agents are dedicated to serving a collective public interest, died from overexposure to better theories and left no heirs. I argue that politicians in a democracy must find ways to dress their actions in public interest clothing. Highly visible special interest benefits just cannot be transferred in the raw.

To make the point, consider these questions. Would the Act to Regulate Commerce that produced the Interstate Commerce Commission in 1887 have passed without the support of Populists who thought they were getting the best of the railroads? Would the English Factory Acts that arguably gave an advantage to capital intensive firms have been passed without the movement against child labor? Would federal meat inspection and the associated limits on the importation of foreign beef have made it on the law books without stories of poisoned food and an associated public outcry? Saying "No" to these questions may be the logical response, but that is not enough.

We need to know more about how an ideological influence becomes valuable in the political economy of regulation. Think about coalitions of groups that support government action where the coalition includes some that seek directly enhanced wealth and others that wish for an improved vision of society.

THE THEORY OF BOOTLEGGERS
AND BAPTISTS

Bootleggers and Baptists have historically supported a form of social regulation that closes corner liquor stores on Sunday. The two groups are distinctive, even though we can refer to their joint effort as forming a coalition. Think about their differences. Bootleggers are generally not accepted in polite Baptist company, certainly not when wearing tags that identify their occupations. Of course, some bootleggers may be Baptist, but the brethren don't advertise that in the Sunday bulletin. Now, consider their common interest—Sunday closing laws that shut down the corner liquor stores. The bootleggers want to eliminate direct competition. The Baptists want to reduce indirect competition and diminish the consumption of alcoholic beverages.

But when we say they both lobby, we must add quickly that the lobbying occurs in markedly different ways. The bootleggers do not organize walks, parades, letter writing campaigns or sit-ins at state capital buildings. They confront the politicians more furtively, yet more positively. The Baptists bring something to the anticompetitive effort that cannot be delivered by bootleggers. They add public interest content to what otherwise would be a strictly private venture. The Baptist element, which I ask you to think of as a generic term, adds a moral ring to what might otherwise be viewed as an immoral effort, the passing of money (and electability) to politicians to obtain a political favor.

Probing deeper into this notion, think about the design of the regulation delivered to bootleggers and Baptists. The common regulation does not consist of higher taxes on alcohol, that is, the use of economic incentives, even though efficiency-driven economists might term that approach the more efficient one. Nor does it address the Sunday consumption or possession of alcoholic beverages. It is command-and-control regulation that focuses solely on the sale of the product. If a diminution in the consumption of the liquid were the overriding goal, a public interest theory would likely predict consumption to be the offense. Going further, a pure public interest argument might conclude that higher taxes on the undesired beverages would address the problem. Of course, monitoring and enforcement costs have to be considered. There is, after all, a supply side to all regulatory problems. But as Becker reminds us, the wealth-redistributing regulation obtained is probably the most efficient in that set; which is to say that both the bootleggers and the Baptists have to be satisfied with the final equilibrium.

Interestingly, regulations of the Sunday sale of booze tie together bootleggers, Baptists, and the legal operators of liquor stores. The bootleggers buy from the legal outlets on Saturday, sell at higher prices on Sunday, and the Baptists praise the effort to enforce the regulatory cartel. Meanwhile, the political suppliers of the regulation reap the support of all the groups, and the Internal Revenue Service works to prevent market entry by those who would produce alcoholic beverages on homemade stills.

What might cause the coalition to crumble, so that we might observe the repeal of Sunday closing laws? To answer that question, we must consider some elements of regulatory demand. First, the Baptist appeal works so long as most of the Baptists recognize and accept the overriding moral argument, so long as the group continues to represent a politically valuable interest group, and so long as group leaders are able to marshal resources from the members. There is always a potential free rider problem in such ventures. What we term the public interest is defined by public opinion, but delivering political support is fraught with practical problems.

Next, the bootleggers must earn a high enough return from their endeavor to buy political favors. If entry occurs in their market—by means of more illicit stills, lower cost transportation from locations that have no restrictions, or by the expansion of lower cost private clubs that offer the restricted beverage to their members, or if demand for the product simply diminishes, the bootleggers will be pushed from the picture. Once the restriction either ceases to be binding or loses its moral support, we predict regulatory reform and the possible replacement of bootleggers by another politically powerful interest group, such as the private club owners.

While bootleggers and Baptists are dominant figures in the theory, there are always other groups who bear the costs of the restriction. They too can become more powerful, especially as the costs of the restriction rise, and can exert enough force to overcome the political demands of the dominant group. Opportunity cost tends always to raise its head.

REGULATORY CASE HISTORIES

An examination of several recent regulatory episodes will illustrate some of these analytical points. Five regulatory stories can be considered: State regulations of Sunday retail sales, or Blue Laws; federal regulation of flammable sleepwear; state regulation of gambling, or lottery laws; a state/federal episode involving seat belts and air bags; and an episode involving control of sulfur dioxide emission.

State Blue Laws

State Blue Laws are kissing cousins of the Sunday Closing Laws that make a market for bootleggers.[7] Both regulations date back to colonial times and reflect religious teachings of the time. Indeed, the term "Blue Law" takes its name from the color of the paper on which early colonial statutes were written. The modern period finds Blue Laws in a gradual state of decline. For example, in 1970, twenty-five states had restrictive statutes. By 1984, only fourteen states remained in the fold, and others were threatening to modify or repeal outright the remaining vestiges of the centuries-old institution. The systematic disappearance of Blue Laws provides an opportunity for researchers to examine the shifting support for the law and so to identify what might motivate the political economy that delivers the rules.

Research on this topic focused on theoretical notions about the demand for Blue Laws and from that developed statistical models that might test the theory. To capture changes in Blue Laws, data for 1970 and 1984 were examined. The theoretical arguments played on the theme of bootleggers and Baptists. We argued that Blue Laws preserve retailers' revenues while distributing those revenues over fewer operating hours and increasing the average per customer purchase. Since their organizing costs are already covered, we argued that unions might be better positioned to bargain for higher wages, though we recognized that most retail establishments are not unionized. We also argued that unionized labor forces have more predictable and uniform work hours and holidays, which means restrictions on Sunday shopping carry lower opportunity costs for unionized communities. Union workers were the first members of the bootlegger group that might favor Blue Laws.

We then thought about bootleggers who might be on the side of repealing Blue Laws. Among various retailers, we predicted large drug stores would fight Sunday restrictions, since they must operate their core businesses on Sunday, have variable costs covered, but are limited by Blue Laws in selling a portion of their inventories defined as "nonessential." On the other hand, we predicted large general retailers would support the laws in the pre-mall 1970 period, since those establishments were geared to compete for downtown shoppers who wouldn't likely flock to the cities on Sundays. In the later period, we predicted large retailers would be either indifferent or opposed to Blue Laws. The large stores might be termed backsliding bootleggers.

The opportunity cost of shopping entered our analysis in another way. Historically, women have specialized in shopping. As the average workers' real wage fell, more women entered the work force, the opportunity cost of Blue Laws rose. The percent of women in the labor force proxied for neither bootleggers nor Baptists, but simply served in our research as an indicator of the cost of the restriction. However, in the earlier period of the analysis, we argued that the widely fractured population of women workers faced a high cost of organizing politically. Later, and due to other causes, women became a more identifiable interest group.

The chief Baptist element in our analysis was the Baptists themselves. We used the percent of the population that were members of the Southern Baptist denomination, an organized interest group that polices free riding with sanctions delivered by conventions, as a proxy for a moral majority that favored Sunday restrictions.

The statistical counterpart of our theory used a "yes, a state has Blue Laws/no, it does not" indicator as the dependent variable and included the arguments mentioned as independent variables. Our statistical findings indicate that the size of the Baptist share of the population has a strong positive association with Blue Laws in 1970, but none in 1984. The Baptist effect seemed to dissipate over time. The percent union is not significant in either period. However, the number of retail stores with more than 100 employees is positively associated with Blue Law status in the 1970 pre-shopping mall period, but has no association in 1984, when larger retail stores were generally found in suburban shopping centers. Drug stores are negatively associated with Blue Laws in 1970, but not associated in 1984.

Briefly stated, we found support for both parts of the theory. Large retail stores and women appear to be bootleggers in the early period. Indeed, work opportunities for women in the early period were associated largely with downtown retail stores and offices. We speculate that having a Sunday holiday appears to have been more important than having opportunities to shop on Sunday. Drug stores bore a cost in the early period, and Baptists played the expected Baptist role. As time passed and the nature of female employment changed, women apparently bore more of the regulation's cost. The Baptist influence, which may have been delivered in large part by women, eroded, and all other significant opposition faded. Blue Laws were repealed.

Flame Resistant Sleepwear

An episode involving the Consumer Product Safety Commission's (CPSC's) 1971 imposition of a flammability regulation for children's sleepwear is particularly interesting, since the agency later, in 1977, banned the chief chemical agent used by industry for meeting the flammability regulation.[8] The chemical, Tris, was found to be a carcinogen.

We learned from an examination of background data that Asian-produced sleepwear had taken a substantial part of the U.S., U.K., Canadian, and European markets prior to the CPSC regulation. The United States and United Kingdom adopted flammability standards at the same time, and foreign penetration of their markets fell markedly. That did not occur in the other developed markets that had no flammability standards. We were suspicious.

In this research, we argued that domestic sleepwear producers gained increased market share from the flammability regulation, but did not likely gain much in the way of profits. Entry is relatively quick and easy in that end of the apparel industry. Thinking more about industry supply curves, we argued that certain producers of synthetic fibers gained from the rules, since cotton fiber and fabric could not meet the CPSC standard. Cotton's market share fell to zero after the regulation. Finally, we argued that the producers of Tris, the chemical selected to meet the standard by virtually all in the yarn and fabric industry, gained from the standard. The product was patented, and five U.S. firms were licensed to produce and market it. They had the most inelastic supply curve of all. Focusing on the demand side, we argued that the demand for the flammability treatment was very inelastic, since it was mandated by law and there were few if any substitutes. That made the burden of the restriction quite palatable.

Although we contend that cotton producers bore the brunt of the industry cost in the episode, we argued they were guarded from losses by a long-standing government-sponsored cartel. The U.S. Department of Agriculture protects cotton producers through acreage and price controls. Perhaps that is partly why a rule destroying a small market for cotton goods could make it through the political thicket.

Using an import penetration model and then financial markets analysis of portfolios of apparel, fabric, fiber, and chemical firms, we tested for effects. The results of the import penetration model provided strong support for the theory that import penetration fell markedly with the imposition of the flammability rule. We also found strong support for the notion of financial gains for fiber and Tris producers. But we found no evidence of gains for apparel and fabric producers, while recognizing that most of the apparel firms were too small to be accounted for in our financial markets tests.

This research suggests the bootleggers were the owners of specialized capital in the chemical and fiber industries. But who were the Baptists? They were the parents of children, and other consumer groups, who pressured the CPSC to develop an all-encompassing flammability standard, a rule that would spread the cost of a desired feature across all consumers in the market. Along these lines, a 1971 report in *Chemical and Engineering News* stated: "An unlikely coalition of mothers and some chemical companies is pleased with the newly promulgated standard."[9] According to our theory, the coalition was not an unlikely one.

Of course, the ban on Tris unraveled all this. Unfortunately, the CPSC rule had the effect of spreading a cancer risk across an entire population of young children. There was an understandable public outcry to the news about Tris. The ban that ended that part of the episode resulted in large financial losses for the chemical industry and smaller ones for the fiber industry. The Tris episode was a case of regulatory failure for all parties, except possibly the political agents who managed it.

The ending of the story illustrates another point: When the bootleggers lose the Baptists, the regulation goes away.

State Regulation of Gambling

Government sponsored gambling can be traced back at least as far as Caesar Augustus, who instituted lotteries for the purpose of rebuilding Rome. They were used by Queen Elizabeth to help fund the Virginia Company's founding of Jamestown. But in more recent times, state-operated lotteries have emerged as a durable source of revenues for state governments.[10]

On its face, gambling is a moral issue to many religious groups. And proposals to institute state lotteries are always opposed by denominational groups. The Baptist element that opposes this state regulation is apparent. That being so, why have lotteries become so popular in recent years? Is this a case like Blue Laws, where moral influence seems to have been swamped by other effects? At present, twenty-eight states have lotteries, up from one in 1964, and their net proceeds in 1986 amounted to more than $5 billion.

Our research on this topic sought to explain state intervention to operate lotteries across states in the face of moral opposition. In our theory, we argued that marginal analyses were made during each legislative session, which is to say that laws could be passed or repealed each year. We first noted that when lottery revenues are viewed as tax revenues, they are highly regressive. Put differently, state-operated lotteries provide an opportunity to transfer income from lower- to higher-income taxpayers, which gives the first bootlegger clue.

We also observed that the ever-present demand for gambling, which is relatively inelastic, can be satisfied by either private or public means, and that private provision occurs legally and illegally. If states are to enter the market successfully, they must find ways to limit their competition. That led us to say that states operating a monopoly lottery will generally have a larger police operation than other states, all else equal.

In the analysis, the demand for repeal, as observed in the nonlottery states, was driven by the Baptist element, which we proxied by the percent of the population holding that faith. Demand for lotteries was driven by higher-income people, proxied by average per capita income, with stronger support coming where state debt per capita was higher and where states had a constitutional requirement for a balanced budget. The number of police, weighted by population, entered the analysis to determine its relationship with lottery status. We also included state taxes per capita in our model that explained the occurrence of lotteries, suggesting that taxes were a substitute for lotteries. The higher those taxes, the less likely a lottery would exist, all else equal.

Focusing on current data in our statistical testing, our estimate found the percent Baptist to be negatively associated with lotteries, debt per capita and income per capita positively related, and police per capita positively related. The presence of a balanced budget requirement was not quite significant, though its sign was positive. We also found state taxes per capita negatively associated with lotteries, which supports the notion that lotteries are a substitute for taxes.

This analysis suggests how other forces can overwhelm a moral element. That is, the bootleggers overwhelmed the Baptists. But we cannot say that Baptists are no longer influential. A related question remains to be resolved. Most states that pass lotteries earmark the funds for some popular social purpose—such as for education. Quite possibly, the bootleggers gain the support of the Baptists by providing an apparent link to a public interest cause that offsets the gambling stigma.

Federally Mandated Air Bags

Another regulatory episode dealt with a very complicated effort by the federal government to mandate the installation of passive restraints in automobiles.[11] The episode began officially in 1969 with an Advance Notice of Proposed Rulemaking issued by the National Highway Safety Administration (NHTSA), followed by a 1971 final rule and a mass of actions, reactions, and delays of implementation; and ending with a 1984 Department of Transportation action requiring states to settle the issue by voting. After two decades, this regulatory issue is still unresolved.

Air bags became a meaningful topic of conversation in the late 1960s when a bulge of people entering the 16–25 age group contributed to a significant increase in auto fatalities. Of course, that was the period when multiple forces contributed to the development of a regulatory binge in Washington, with many new agencies being formed, additional laws passed, and thousands of new regulations placed on the books.

The air bag had been used to protect test pilots in the development of aircraft, and one of the bag manufacturers approached NHTSA about requiring that the device be used in all new automobiles. They believed air bags would protect drivers who chose not to use seat belts.

Interest in air bags increased, and Ford Motor Company joined Eaton Manufacturing Company to demonstrate the first working air bag at an engineering society meeting in early 1968. Soon thereafter, Ford became discouraged about the bag's prospects, noting serious problems for out-of-position passengers and the probability that passengers would be seriously injured by inflating bags. It was also clear that seat belts still would be needed in combination with bags to meet the rules NHTSA was contemplating.

General Motors then became the leading proponent for air bags and demonstrated its ability to build bag-equipped autos early on. With that, NHTSA proposed its passive restraint rule, and GM indicated it would strive to meet the standard with air bags. The other major auto producers sued NHTSA. Eventually much more was learned about air bags, auto safety, and the consumers' willingness to buy bag-equipped cars. Along the way, Sam Peltzman shook the cage of safety scholars with his finding that cars equipped with safety equipment could induce a lulling effect that caused drivers to sustain more instead of fewer injuries.[12] That did not slow the regulatory juggernaut, but other political and market events did.

Who were the supporters of air bags? Obviously, the holders of air bag patents. But the auto insurance industry was the strongest and most persistent advocate of all. Why so? Surely, other groups interested in safety and health would be counted first.

Auto insurers can gain from passive restraints in several ways. First, the insurers could determine risk easier where passive restraints are used. Unlike belts, the mere presence of bags insures protection to the head and upper body in the event of a head-on accident. Second, they could earn one-time gains from contracts written on the basis of higher risks, which would be reduced by the installation of passive restraints. Third, a reduction in head-related injuries—the most expensive of all—would reduce the cost of extensive injury-related litigation, which would reduce price and expand markets. In addition to these reasons for supporting the regulation, as a regulated industry, insurance firms could gain demand for their product by means of the publicity accompanying a long and controversial regulatory proceeding and encounter little competitive response in doing so.

Along with the insurance firms, General Motors was a potential winner, at least in the beginning of the episode. Its competition was behind in developing bag-equipped cars. A rule requiring bags would raise competitors' costs.

Who were the Baptists? All those who responded to the promise of safer cars and reduced fatalities. As some might put it, how could anyone be opposed to auto safety? Ralph Nader's

Center for Auto Safety, funded largely by the auto insurance industry, was chief among the organizations that prompted this support.

Financial markets analysis was used to estimate abnormal returns for portfolios of auto manufacturers, air bag manufacturers, and insurance firms. The analytical approach forms a portfolio of the relevant stocks and compares its performance to the entire New York Stock Exchange's performance in association with specific events. Sudden changes in the returns to the portfolio relative to the exchange are then identified. In all, ten key events might have increased or decreased the wealth of the portfolio shareholders as the rules were imposed, delayed, modified, and finally put to state vote. While there were mixed results for a number of the events, we observed that air bag producers gained substantial wealth when the passive restraint rule was introduced. Ford and Chrysler suffered cumulative losses, but neither GM nor AMC suffered a loss in association with the initial rule.

When NHTSA delayed the rule in 1970, both the insurance industry and air bag portfolios sustained abnormal losses. However, the delay did not generate gains for the auto portfolio, partly because the delay was accompanied by additional safety standards that related to padding and interior design. In 1980 Congress again passed legislation delaying the standard but required passive restraints to be met by producers of smaller cars first—a barrier to the flood of imported cars. On that occasion, both the automakers and air bag producers experienced abnormal gains.

In other work, we examined the later state votes on mandatory seat belts, which could result in the elimination of passive restraint requirements. A vote for mandatory belts was a vote against mandatory passive restraints. Our estimating equation for explaining whether or not a mandatory seat belt referendum was passed, using 1986 data, showed that the number of automobiles produced in a state was positively associated with passage. By the time of the vote, auto producers were generally opposed to passive restraints. Earlier efforts to market bags had not been successful and the required installation of passive restraints in smaller cars would significantly raise price. The presence of an air bag manufacturer in a state had strong negative partial effects, and the number of employees in a state's fire, marine, and casualty insurance sector, weighted by population, was negatively associated with passage of mandatory seat belt laws. They wanted passive restraints.

In terms of bootleggers and Baptists, the passive restraint research suggests that auto insurance companies, the producers of air bags, and at one point, the leading auto producer were early bootleggers. Public interest groups took the moral high ground and gained financial support from some bootleggers. As time passed and import penetration increased, a carefully molded passive restraint rule was seen as a way to restrain competition. The ranks of the bootleggers increased and moved in lockstep with the Baptists.

Eventually, belts and bags competed in a political economy with bootleggers and Baptists. Meanwhile, technology advanced, prices of passive restraints fell, and more producers began to offer the item as standard equipment in higher-priced cars.

Control of Sulfur Dioxide Emissions

From the very outset of the environmental saga, control of sulfur dioxide emissions has been a matter of high priority.[13] The problem is as old as the burning of naturally formed fuel. The uncontrolled burning of coal and petroleum products generates oxides of the sulfur that is contained in the fuels. A standard for sulfur dioxide emissions was one of the first developed by EPA.

Any emission standard that has meaningful effects cuts into the production plans of polluters. In this case, electricity production was the product most affected. Tight sulfur dioxide limits quickly became limits on industrial and residential growth in the affected regions. Because of political pressures generated by states that sought more economic development, Congress debated whether or not to give state governors the power to intervene when EPA standards appeared to be too constraining.

The research on sulfur dioxide control examined one very small chapter in the regulatory history of this particular pollutant. The study focused on 1977 congressional efforts to amend the 1970 Clean Air Act. At the time, there were two competing amendments involving sulfur dioxide. Both allowed for variances in the tight emission standard, so that major construction and other seasonal activities would not be blocked by the rule. But one amendment gave state governors the power to allow for variances. The other gave that power to the EPA. The central question had to do with state versus federal control. The research involved an examination of the votes taken in Congress in an effort to identify the determinants of the votes themselves.

In doing the work, I assumed that environmentalists preferred federal control of emission variances. It is less costly for national lobby groups to influence one set of federal regulators than many sets at the state level. I also expected that proponents of industrial growth would favor state control. After all, state governors are sensitive to economic growth, tax revenues that spring from it, and the pressure they feel from groups who seek better jobs and incomes. This does not say that state governors are immune to environmental concerns, but that the pressures of industrial growth are more apparent to them than to Washington regulators.

I analyzed the votes statistically by building a model that predicted the share of a state's delegation that voted in favor of state control. Variables included in the model to explain that share were the percent of the state population that lived in regions with high sulfur dioxide emission levels; the percent of the work force employed in the five heavy polluting industries; and the recent growth rate of manufacturing by state.

I expected the sulfur dioxide variable to be positively associated with federal control, if environmentalists were truly sensitive to pollution levels. I also expected the employment variable to favor state control, since jobs were at stake and state governors would be more sensitive to local employment problems. I predicted industrial growth would be positively associated with state control, since the proponents for growth have more to offer state governors than federal regulators. The results confirmed these predictions, except in the case of employment, which was not a significant factor in explaining the vote.

Going on in the analysis, I sought to determine just what influenced the environmentalists in the vote, since the effect of high sulfur dioxide emissions favored federal regulation. Were the environmentalists motivated primarily by concern over the emissions, or was it opposition to industrial growth? That was the next question.

To get at that question, a statistical test was developed using the League of Conservation Voters index for state delegations to Congress, where the League gives an overall rating on the delegations' sensitivity to environmental issues. The population living in high sulfur emission locations, the level of employment in polluting industries, and industrial growth were again used as variables to explain the League index. If the League index reflected environmental concerns, I expected the sulfur dioxide variable to be strongly positive. On the other hand, if the environmentalist record reflected opposition to industry, not direct concern for environmental quality, that variable would not be important. The others would.

I found sulfur dioxide emissions were not significant in explaining the League index. Industrial growth was a strong, negative determinant. Employment offered no explanatory power. The result suggests the environmental movement was more about stopping industry than stopping pollution, at least in this case.

To probe deeper, I included the League of Conservation Voters index in the first model, the one that explained the votes. In that case, the League index overpowered the industrial growth variable, simply reflecting the same effect. None of the other variables were significantly affected.

What does this say about bootleggers and Baptists and competing visions? The empirical findings suggest that the environmental movement was used by those who wanted to slow down economic development in their regions. The movement was not directly concerned with reductions in pollution per se. That was an instrument for achieving another goal.

Who might gain from reduction in development? Owners of existing resorts, fishermen, hunters, and others who enjoy nature unaffected by homes, schools, hospitals, and industrial plants. The bootleggers are those who have special interests that benefit from reductions in growth, including some pure environmentalists. The Baptists are those who support anything that has a good environmental ring to it. In this case, it was sulfur dioxide emission reduction.

CONCLUDING THOUGHTS

The theory of bootleggers and Baptists argues that competing visions matter in the political economy of regulation, but they matter in a very specific way. When considering the effective demand for regulation and the final form taken by specific rules, we must look for an important group of demanders who deliver public interest content to the regulatory cause. In the first place, there is considerable competition for political favors, and a politician must be able to explain his actions. That being so, we should expect to find strong public interest statements about the virtues of regulation that can be ratified by important social groups and figures.

We should recognize that groups like the Environmental Defense Fund and the Sierra Club, to name two, are vital to the passage of clean air legislation. We should also recognize that the support of those groups can be quite valuable to polluters who seek a particular form of regulation, a form that may raise their competitors' costs or in other ways improve the future profits of an industry group.

The struggle for regulation that best serves the bootlegger-Baptist coalition occurs at the federal level. It is difficult to gain very much in a competitive environment across fifty states. In a similar way, the outcomes predicted by the theory seldom apply to actions taken by courts. The theory best explains legislative and regulatory actions where the political process can be affected through lobbying, campaign contributions, and efforts by politicians to satisfy constituent groups.

The evolution of environmental regulation in the United States allows us to observe just how much a special interest theory of regulation might explain. In the chapters to follow, direct references will be made to interest groups' struggles, but while it may be apparent from the stories, members of the groups will seldom be referred to directly as "bootleggers" or "Baptists."

NOTES

1. This chapter is based on a paper presented at the Broyhill Forum, Appalachian State University, Boone, North Carolina, November 11, 1988. For proceedings of the Forum, see Bruce Yandle, "Bootleggers and Baptists in the Market for Regulation," in *The Political Economy of Government Regulation*, ed. by Jason F. Shogren (Norwell, Mass.: Kluwer Academic Publishers, forthcoming.)

2. See Richard A. Posner, "Theories of Economic Regulation," *Bell Journal* 5 (autumn 1974), 335–58.

3. See Sam Peltzman, "Toward a More General Theory of Regulation," *Journal of Law and Economics*, 19 (August 1976), 211–40, and George J. Stigler, "The Theory of Economic Regulation," *Bell Journal* (spring 1971), 3–21.

4. See Gordon Tullock, "The Welfare Costs of Tariffs, Monopolies, and Theft," *Western Economic Journal*, 5 (June 1967), 224–32, and James M. Buchanan, "Rent Seeking and Profit Seeking," in *Toward a Theory of the Rent-Seeking Society*, ed. by J.M. Buchanan, R.D. Tollison, and Gordon Tullock (College Station: Texas A&M Press, 1980).

5. See Fred S. McChesney, "Rent Extraction and Rent Creation in the Economic Theory of Regulation," *The Journal of Legal Studies*, vol. 16 (1987), 101–17.

6. See Gary S. Becker, "A Theory of Competition Among Pressure Groups for Political Influence," *The Quarterly Journal of Economics*, vol. 118, no. 3 (August 1983), 371–99.

7. This discussion is drawn from Jamie Price and Bruce Yandle, "Labor Markets and Sunday Closing Laws," *Journal of Labor Research*, 8 (fall 1987), 407–13.

8. This section is drawn from Gordon Shuford and Bruce Yandle, "Consumer Protection, Private Interest Effects, and Government Liability: The Tris Episode," unpublished manuscript, Department of Economics, Clemson University, 1988.

9. See "Flammability Rule Argued," *Chemical and Engineering News* (April 9, 1971), 9.

10. This section is based on Robert Martin and Bruce Yandle, "Lotteries as Transfer Mechanisms," unpublished manuscript, Department of Economics, Clemson University, 1988.

11. This section is based on Robert A. Kneuper, "The Political Economy of Mandatory Passive Restraints: An Investigation of Auto Safety Regulation," Master's thesis, Department of Economics, Clemson University, 1987.

12. See Sam Peltzman, "The Effects of Automobile Safety Regulation," *Journal of Political Economy*, 83 (August–December 1975), 677–725. For more on this, see Robert Crandall, *Regulating the Automobile* (Washington: Brookings Institution, 1986).

13. This discussion is based on Bruce Yandle, "Sulfur Dioxide: State versus Federal Control," *The Journal of Energy and Development*, vol. 10, no. 1 (autumn 1984), 63–69.

3

Environmental Protection Before Federal Regulation

INTRODUCTION

Contrary to what might be thought by a typical college student born in 1970, environmental regulation in the United States did not begin with the formation of the EPA that same year. Government regulation of air, water quality, and noise at the state and local level goes back centuries. The problem is as old as man. Concentration of production and consumption leads to concentrated wastes that must in some way be disposed of or controlled.

Moving away from the problem offers one solution. People offended by noxious fumes and producers that require high quality water as an input can move when things get unbearable. Bringing suit for damages or to enjoin the polluter's action is another possible option. When the cost of moving or suing begins to exceed the cost of affecting the polluter's behavior in other ways, more detailed rules of property emerge and are enforced. Restrictive covenants are incorporated in deeds; private actions are taken in courts, and public actions are taken in passing zoning, noise, and smoke control ordinances.

The somewhat random drift of economic development suggests that every city and state will not face the same pollution problems at the same time. Industrial development tends to become concentrated in some regions, while others enter the development process more slowly. Yet even if pollution is the same in several geographic and political regions, there is no reason that the individuals who face the problem will all agree on its magnitude or that something should be done about it.

The relative value people assign to improvements in environmental quality is lower in some areas than the benefits obtained by devoting the same resources to some other endeavor. Values and relative scarcity vary across communities.

The nation's historical experience bears this out. The older industrialized regions faced pollution problems first. They passed laws to change things. People in newer, less industrialized locations, and therefore less polluted ones, consciously made other tradeoffs. In some cases, they chose to seek income through industrial development, foregoing the use of strict environmental regulations in order to reduce the cost of industrial development.

In other cases, the pollution accepted in one location sometimes drifted to other locations that then bore the costs of their own pollution and that of their upstream neighbors. To deal with the forces of gravity and wind currents as the nation shifted from being a mainly agricultural society to an industrial society, state laws gradually supplanted local ordinances, and then regional compacts emerged.

The different regulatory environments that emerged arguably reflect the desires of people—the consumers, workers, and owners of assets in the various locations. As expected under representative government, some local and state groups were treated less favorably than others. But there was a safeguard. Firms could adjust their locations as they searched for the best combination of desired benefits. Minority groups that wanted either extreme levels of purity or dirt were disciplined by competition across locations and the relatively free movement of resources. The political-economic struggle that ensued tended to balance forces that called for one degree of control or another.

During the period, federalism offered the benefits of experimentation by discovering alternative solutions to the pollution problem. There was a trial and error approach of the sort recently praised by Aaron Wildavsky for its association with innovations and strong competitive incentives to reduce cost.[1] But while the resulting diversity may have satisfied the

heterogeneous interests of the American population and arguably yielded lower-cost solutions to the control problem, the
result created problems for groups with other interests.

Firms located in a highly polluted location, one with stricter
state laws, for example, frequently had to compete with firms
in a less polluted location where there were lax standards.
Competitive problems grew with expanding national markets.
But the expanded geographic markets made it easier for plants
to relocate in more favorable regulatory climates.

Plants expanding in locations that assigned a relatively low
priority to pollution control could reduce regulatory costs, but
relocation was costly on other grounds. Workers with higher
wage contracts, politicians with specialized knowledge about
particular constituent groups, older cities with fragile tax bases, and individuals who just didn't want to move or lose a
somewhat stable social structure, opposed the growth of industry in newer regions.

Those who wanted a cleaner environment that could be paid
for by a vast body of consumers and taxpayers argued for environmental protection in the form of a uniform baseline to
be met eventually at all locations (national standards). There
were competing visions about how to address the problem and
competing interest groups sometimes agreed that government
action should be taken. As we will see, these are elements of a
refrain to be repeated throughout the environmental saga.

This chapter traces the development of pollution regulation
from ancient times to the very early common law remedies
on to the more encompassing state legislation and regional
compacts that emerged in the pre-federal period. The cases
discussed and experience recounted illustrate variety, social
learning, but also underline the effects of various interest
groups who struggled in political economies to alter the use
of the environment.

THE EARLY YEARS: COMMON LAW
REMEDIES

Certainly there have been many environmental problems in
the history of man as well as in the recent history of our nation.

In 1908, for example, an observer discussed the City of New York and described its population of 120,000 horses as an "economic burden, an affront to cleanliness, and a terrible tax on human life."[2] With unwitting optimism, the writer suggested that the solution to the urban air pollution problem would come through technological change—the introduction of the horseless carriage. As was often the case, one form of pollution was later exchanged for another. Put differently, CO replaced BO.

The 15,000 horses in Rochester, New York, described by the same writer, annually produced enough manure to form a pile 175 feet high covering an acre of land. There was some satisfaction to be found in living in a one-horse town during those days. There was even noise pollution legislation as early as 1785. That year, New York City passed an ordinance forbidding teams and wagons with iron-shod wheels from driving on the streets.

If one goes back far enough, it seems eventually there would be no laws or regulations dealing specifically with environmental pollution. But the search would have to extend beyond 1307 when Edward I issued an order prohibiting the burning of sea coal in a smelter near London.[3] The order requiring that the operator avoid the use of high-sulfur coal somehow sounds familiar.

(W)hereas smelters were accustomed to make their fires of firewood or charcoal, they now more than usual make them of sea coal, whereby an intolerable stench diffuses itself in the neighborhood and infects the air, in consequence whereof the king commanded the mayor and sheriffs in London and the sheriffs of Middlesex and Surrey to make a proclamation that all persons wishing to exercise that mystery should cease to use coal, the ordinance is not observed; and they are to punish offenders by grievous ransoms.[4]

America did not adopt such statutes in its colonial history, since industrial development was practically precluded by the mother country. Those statutes came later, much later. Instead, the young nation relied on the use of common law remedies, a legal framework inherited from England.[5] The history of those actions points to two levels of attack. The first is private action by a plaintiff, which reflected a rule of property.

In those actions, the individual bringing suit claims that his right to the use of his property has been eliminated by the defendant's actions. The suit claims that property has been taken. The second level of attack is seen in public nuisance complaints. In the first category of cases, individuals who claim to be damaged by another party must prove their private losses are associated with the other party's use of his property. The controversy lies between two well-identified parties. However, if the alleged harm is widespread, only a governmental body can bring action for an injunction against the polluter. What might at first appear to be a private action can become a public nuisance case.

Since the late 1800s, pollution damage has been viewed more frequently as causing public rather than private harm. Even so, the use of private complaints offered certain desirable characteristics for resolving pollution problems. The point is illustrated in the much earlier but frequently cited William Alfred's common law case of 1611.[6] In the case, a homeowner complained about a pig farmer who built a pigsty so close to the plaintiff's home that he could no longer enjoy the expected pleasures of his own residence.

Siding with the plaintiff, the court attempted to balance benefits and costs, discussed the air pollution nuisance, and then enjoined the farm from disturbing the right to a healthful home. A rule of reason was introduced by the court, one which considered the various alternatives available to the parties.

In a much later case (1904), *Madison v. Ducktown Sulphur, Copper, and Iron Co.*, Ducktown Copper Company had polluted a large area around Copperhill, Tennessee, and had ruined the land for continuation of farming, an activity that preceded the operation of the copper smelter. When confronted with the case, the court sided with the copper company, saying essentially that the combined wealth of the community would be larger if the copper mine continued to operate. Again, the court sought the least cost avoider of the problem. There were lower cost alternatives for farmers than for copper companies.[7]

While the courtroom was a place for resolving conflicts over the use of property, it was also a place where new environmental principles were stated. Along with balancing the equities, making efforts to maximize the value of community assets, and resolving questions of private versus public harm, the courts developed the defense of "coming to the nuisance." An individual who purchased land at a location that was already polluted could not turn and bring action against the polluter.

Viewed in another way, property rights to continue emitting waste at some constant level were endowed to the polluter. Arguably, the value of land in the vicinity of the polluter was already depreciated by the polluter's action at the time it was purchased by the late arriver. To allow the new land owner to then bring suit and recover would generate windfall gains and encourage extortion through the courts.

Public Nuisance

The doctrine of public nuisance arguably evolved for two reasons. First, environmental assets became scarcer, but clear-cut property rights to their use were not defined and enforced. The government did not claim the scarce asset and treat it with ownerlike concern, and individuals could not make such claims without some enforcement of their rights by government. The environment existed as a common-access resource long after conflicting uses generated problems.

Crowding of the environment meant that well-identified but diverse groups of people were either harmed or benefited when their intended use of the environment prevailed over some other group's desired use. For example, farmers, merchants, and some manufacturers might sustain harm from the upstream discharge of wastes into a river. In a similar way, a large number of people and their physical property might be adversely affected by the burning of coal in large furnaces.

Instead of a few easily identifiable parties suffering damage and bringing suit, as in the early common law cases, many widely separated parties felt the effects. Multiple sources of pollution that affected identifiable groups also emerged. There were large numbers on both sides of the transaction.

In this setting, the typically slow and cumbersome court-room battles were costly. Local ordinances began to develop. As illustrated in *People v. Detroit White Lead Works* (1890), coming to the nuisance was no longer a defense. Victor Yannacone and Bernard Cohen touch on the evolving pattern of controls discussed earlier and summarize the case.

As the community started to grow and people lived closer to the plant, they began to suffer headaches, nausea and vomiting from the odors, smoke and soot which was emitted from the plant. The Court rejected the contention of the defendants that they were there first, saying "The defendant cannot be protected in the enjoyment of their property and the carrying on of their business if it becomes a nuisance to people living upon the adjoining properties ... Whenever such a business becomes a nuisance it must either devise some means to avoid the nuisance or remove or cease the business. Nor is it of any consequence that the business is a useful one or necessary or that it contributes to the welfare and prosperity of the community."[8]

In effect, the court transferred the right to the environment from the producer of lead to the community at large. A broad public interest logic displaced the weighing of community benefits and costs observed in *Ducktown Copper*.

Legislative action by city governments appears to be the next step observed in the legal treatment of the environment. The balancing of benefits and costs done by judges was transferred to politicians. In the case of *Bowers v. Indianapolis* (1907), the Supreme Court of Indiana upheld the Indianapolis city ordinance declaring smoke a public nuisance. The court's opinion spoke to the evolving large numbers problem and addressed the appropriateness of legislative actions for dealing with pollution.

The question we have to deal with is not as to the authority to regulate the emission of dense smoke in a sparsely inhabited locality, wherein the act could only result in the creation of a private nuisance, but ... within ... a populous city, ... thereby impairing the health and comfort of thousands(.) If there is anything in the principle of the greatest good to the greatest number, or in the declared authority of government reasonably to regulate the use of property for the common good, it must be affirmed that power exists to deal

with a condition which renders life in a great manufacturing city little short of impossible. These considerations make general restrictive
regulations permissible, presenting, as they do, a case in which the
discretion of the municipal legislature is invoked to determine whether . . . a general regulation is required.[9]

But not every state court arrived at the same conclusion. Nor
did every city adopt ordinances at the same time. Different circumstances and public opinion regarding the relative merits of
pollution were reflected when legal actions surfaced. In other
words, experimentation was reflected across states. Individuals
seeking to relocate a plant or a home could consider a large
array of options and choose the one that best suited their preferences.

A 1935 Pennsylvania case provides an interesting contrast
to the earlier Indianapolis case and illustrates clearly how
circumstances of time and place were recognized in common
law actions. *Versailles Burrough v. McKessport Coal and Coke
Company* involved the burning of coal slag near Pittsburgh.
The action occurred during the depths of the Great Depression, a time when many people were happy to see smokestacks
fuming. Siding with the coal company, the judge wrote:

Much of economic distress is due to the fact that there is not enough
smoke in Pittsburgh and the Pittsburgh district. The metropolis that
earned the sobriquet of the "smokey city" has not been living up to
those vaporous laurels. The economic activity of the city that was
known as "the workshop of the world" has decreased in proportion
as its skies cleared of smoke. While smoke *per se* is objectionable and
adds nothing to the other aesthetics of any community, it is not without its connotational beauty as it rises in clouds from smoke stacks or
furnaces and ovens . . . telling the world that the fires of prosperity
are burning—the fires assure economic security to the workingman, as
well as establish profitable returns on capital legitimately invested.[10]

Settling environmental disputes through the courts was
slower than actions taken under an ordinance, but the courts
offered something unique. They could provide needed flexibility when community circumstances seemed to call for that.

The Development of Local Air Pollution Ordinances

Just as they did much later in the 1970s and 1980s, public opinion and public interest organizations had early impact in evolving environmental laws and regulations. As mentioned before, city and municipal ordinances existed early in the United States. For example, Chicago passed a smoke abatement ordinance in 1861. Pittsburgh did the same in 1917, following some interesting and effective action by a civic group, which had formed in 1890. That year, a Health Protection Association was formed by private Pittsburgh citizens.

In an effort to become informed advocates of improved environmental quality, members of the group visited a smokeless furnace operating in an industrial plant and then prepared a press story on its economic advantages.[11] After that, the association focused on health-related issues and became so successful that it formed the Civic Club of Allegheny County as a vehicle for seeking air quality improvements. Prominent city leaders joined the movement, and they were instrumental in forming a city bureau of smoke regulation and the passage of a 1917 city ordinance.[12] The vision of control by expert authorities overcame the vision of control by property rights and common law remedies.

A flurry of similar local activity occurred across the country in the 1940s. St. Louis enacted an ordinance in 1940, Providence in 1947. Indeed, in 1950 it was reported that all but four U.S. cities with a population of 250,000 or more had some type of air pollution control ordinance.[13] At the time, two states—New Jersey and Pennsylvania—were debating pending state legislation.

City ordinances typically required periodic furnace inspections, the registration of suppliers of fuel and furnace equipment, smoke standards, permits for new construction, penalties of violators, and an appeal procedure. To illustrate, the 1940 St. Louis ordinance proscribed the use of soft coal unless it was used with a mechanical stoker or the volatile content of the coal had been reduced.[14]

Though concern about property damage was an important element in explaining the early ordinances, public health issues always seemed to drive the system that delivered the rules. After the St. Louis ordinance was in place, observers reported a 40 percent decrease in respiratory infections. A 1949 Chicago-Cook County health survey estimated air pollution damages at $35 million, or $10 per capita. Early discussion of the benefits and costs of polluting activities show clearly that these considerations were important.

Tracing the development of air pollution regulations in Pittsburgh helps to illustrate how local flexibility was exercised and then translated into control by a larger political jurisdiction. After a severe bout with pollution in the winter of 1940–41, which resulted in citizens wearing gauze masks and the city operating streetlights in midday, the citizens of Pittsburgh took steps to update its 1917 ordinance.

However, after raising the penalties for discharging smoke, Pittsburgh officials realized their actions alone could not solve the problem. Drifting smoke did not recognize political boundaries, and many large industrial plants had located out of the city, perhaps to escape the city's various pollution ordinances. Where in the past, there were problems when a person came to the nuisance and then complained, in the Pittsburgh case, the nuisance had moved, but the ordinance followed.

Expansion of the population and economic activity to be included in a uniform regulatory framework understandably brings problems. The problem is familiar. What works for a relatively homogeneous population of people and activities becomes uncomfortable as heterogeneity increases. Shifting pollution controls from lower to higher levels of government is comparable to expanding membership in a cartel. Agreement comes easier when the membership is small, shares the same goals, and has relatively similar production costs. Difficulties emerge when people who previously rejected the cartel are pressured to join.

After the Pittsburgh city officials placed pressure on the Allegheny County Commission, urging them to adopt a uniform air pollution ordinance patterned after the city's, the county complied, but not without a struggle. Industrial and labor leaders mounted an effort to blunt the action. Slogans and phrases were repeated in newspaper stories and speeches: "Smoke means prosperity," "Smokeless chimneys mean hungry children."[15] As always, cleaner air was not a free good. One man's pollution was symbolic of another's economic opportunity.

APPROACHES TAKEN BY OTHER CITIES, COUNTIES, AND STATES

After experiencing more than twenty years of federal environmental regulation since the late 1960s that is characterized by uniform rules to be met by each and every political jurisdiction, it is difficult to appreciate what was lost when state and local governments could no longer develop their own unique approaches for dealing with pollution. The pre-federal period of control is like a gigantic social laboratory with many competing experiments underway, where each experiment reflects the desires of the affected people as expressed in their own political economy.

The development of water quality regulation in the state of Massachusetts, and particularly along the Merrimack River, serves to illustrate the point.[16] Activities at the state level began in 1887 with the passage of water control legislation that focused on public health concerns and required that surveys be taken and rivers classified as to use. As a result of that action, all rivers in Massachusetts were classified as to industrial or recreational use, with the latter rivers maintained as trout streams.

Instead of requiring uniform standards, people in the state apparently allowed for cost-effective use of its streams. The Merrimack, Blackstone, and Neponset rivers were classified as industrial streams. These three rivers were actually waste disposal streams for industrial plants and were not to be used under any circumstances for the supply of drinking water or for recreational purposes.

The classification system seemed to have worked. In 1936 a special Massachusetts health commission reviewed the earlier decision and reported that the industrial streams were "of great industrial value and their use for this purpose has contributed to the prosperity of the Commonwealth. Although the Commission does not wish to condone willful defilement of any stream, it believes that the most that can be expected in such cases is that the manufacturers use all practicable means to prevent pollution."[17]

Some of the thoughts expressed by the commission sound familiar as we reflect on the evolution of federal laws and the outpouring of federal tax moneys to state and local governments that came later, but the important point here is the flexibility and innovation that was occurring at the state and local level in finding fiscally acceptable solutions to the pollution problem.

The story about the Merrimack indicates that towns and cities along the industrial stream accepted the classification and then supported continuation of industrial status, with one major exception. That was the town of Newburyport, located at the mouth of the Merrimack. It received the accumulated discharge of all the upstream towns and industrial plants. However, the city took action to solve its problem by installing water treatment facilities. Of course, there was no way to charge the upstream dischargers for the cost of removing their discharge.

From post–World War II to the middle 1960s, residents of cities along the Merrimack expressed strong preferences for keeping the industrial status of the river. There were no health problems. Drinking water was available from other sources, and industry in the region, which was generally declining for competitive reasons, was able to operate longer without incurring high waste treatment costs. When referenda for bond issues to fund improved waste treatment facilities were proposed, they were systematically defeated. There was a revealed willingness to accept the environmental control scheme of the region.

It was not until the federal government entered the water quality picture that Massachusetts accepted payment from the larger U.S. tax base and revised its management of the Merrimack. Even then there were serious questions about the actual need for improved water quality. The rivers had been able to assimilate wastes and meet the preferences of the population in the basin. But cheap federal dollars alter the relative costs of environmental quality. The price of water quality went down and more was demanded. As George Downey summarized the change that arrived, "Recent state and federal legislation and policy have all but obliterated (the local) threshold of action. Current policy warrants water pollution control at any cost, contending that no one has the right to pollute. The basis for action is no longer a physically self-evident situation and this strains credulity of (Merrimack) valley residents."[18]

Variety in approaches taken by states to resolve pollution problems is also seen in the pre-federal California experience. The state's 1947 Air Pollution Control Act grandfathered all existing polluters and set emission standards that were seldom uniform across regions.[19] New York offers yet another example of diversity. In 1964, the State Department of Health divided the state into four classified regions, much like a typical zoning map.[20] There were industrial, commercial, residential, and rural classifications, with the rural areas having higher air quality standards.

Regulation of air quality in Texas came after it was recognized that federal rules were on the way.[21] The state's 1965 statute established an Air Control Board, which was instructed to clean up pollution "consistent with maximum employment and full industrial development of the state."[22] As might be expected, the state encountered difficulties when it attempted to displace city and county regulations. In 1967, the state legislature deprived local governments of the right to regulate air pollution, wherever local ordinance conflicted with state law.

Interestingly, one special interest group successfully gained an exemption when the state became the monopoly regulator. The cotton ginning industry and all others that process agricultural products in their natural state were placed outside the law. The success of those industries could well reflect the cost advantage that comes from lobbying one state legislature as opposed to seeking to influence many city and county governments.

While special interest groups always seem to influence the shape and form of regulation, the variety of that influence is expected to be subject to more competition when multiple governments are involved in dealing with pollution. Firms that are mobile can move to locations that place higher values on employment and tax revenues than on environmental quality. If one county has stricter rules, firms expanding plants may easily locate in an adjoining county with more favorable rules. When regulation drifts to the state level, the cost of moving to another location rises. And when regulation moves ultimately to the federal level, all options are closed.

DEALING WITH THE INTERSTATE POLLUTION PROBLEM

As pollution became more widespread across political jurisdictions and people with common concerns about the problem, the cost of developing legal structures for resolving questions of benefits, costs, who should pay, and how to collect, became greater. In the face of that problem, state compacts offered a solution. The history of the Ohio River Valley Sanitation Commission (ORANSCO), an organization established in 1948 that eventually included the states of Illinois, Indiana, Kentucky, Ohio, Pennsylvania, Virginia, and West Virginia, illustrates a successful interstate effort to manage environmental quality.[23]

In ways reminiscent of Pittsburgh's first effort to control air pollution, ORANSCO began in 1935 when Cincinnati's Chamber of Commerce began to push for pollution control in their city and throughout the entire Ohio River basin. The chamber had good reasons to be concerned about the city's environmental future. In a way, Cincinnati was the septic tank of the Ohio basin. Located at the lower end of the Ohio River, Cincinnati received the wastes of 19 million people and some of the world's largest industrial plants. Even if the city had operated sufficient sewage treatment facilities for its own population, there was little it could do alone to put a significant dent in the growing water pollution problems.

The effects of upstream waste discharge were so dominant in the eight-state basin that in 1908 the Ohio legislature had exempted every village and city along the river from installing sewage treatment facilities until those upstream had taken action. The law of gravity was determining the outcome. But it took more than political pleadings to bring about a reverse domino effect. Those far enough upstream felt no costs from their actions until 1931 when a long period of low water flow brought an epidemic of gastroenteritis that reversed the effects of gravity. The infection moved upstream. That, and an outbreak of typhoid in 1936, provided the necessary impetus to do something other than treat the river as a common-access resource. Mother Nature sent bills to the upstream dischargers.

Cincinnati took decisive action in 1938 when citizens passed a $1 million bond issue for the construction of a sewage treatment plant. But it was still difficult to persuade upstream industrial dischargers to alter their behavior. During a 1935 session of the Pennsylvania legislature in hearings on water pollution control, an industrialist met with a committee and indicated support for the concept of cleaning up the river. Having said that, he quickly added that the cost of controls would place the state's industry at a competitive disadvantage with firms located elsewhere.[24] Much later, the same industrialist appeared before the U.S. Senate Commerce Committee, which was discussing pollution control, and again avowed support for clean water. In this case, however, the industrialist indicated the federal government had no business telling Pennsylvania how to manage its internal affairs. Implicitly, the industrialist was calling for uniform controls across all industries, if pollution rules were to be adopted.

The eight states that formed the ORANSCO compact eventually set the pace of progressive pollution control programs. Even though the struggle to bring the states together took twelve years, partly because of the intervention of World War II, the compact organization eventually established water quality standards for municipal waste treatment, and process standards were accepted for all the basin's industrial plants. In each case, the standards were related to ambient water quality. They were not uniform across dischargers. The emphasis was on improving the quality of the environment, not on the quality of the machinery in plants.

By 1960, ORANSCO had robot monitors giving automatic readings of ten different water quality measurements throughout the basin. In 1965, the monitoring system was complete. And by 1967, some 90 percent of the 1,700 direct dischargers to the river had complied with ORANSCO minimum treatment standards, and 94 percent of the region's population was connected to sewers served by municipal treatment plants. Capital expenditures for sewage treatment facilities then totaled $1 billion, of which 90 percent was locally financed.

ORANSCO was not the only river management system to use robot monitoring and permitting. Having passed its first water pollution control legislation in 1903, the state of New York went on to establish a discharge permit system that in 1949 required approval of all new and modified sources of pollution.[25] Like Ohio's, New York's problem stemmed primarily from the discharge of municipal waste. Finally, after a $1 billion bond referendum in 1965, New York citizens took up the challenge to construct new sewage treatment plants across the state. With growing improvements in the volume of untreated waste discharged into rivers, the state developed a system of water quality monitors and by 1975 was able to obtain continuous readouts of water quality for every 200 miles of river water in the state.

Other ORANSCO-like regional compacts emerged in the pre-federal period. Indeed, just prior to the migration of pollution control to the federal level, states along the Tennessee River were negotiating a similar arrangement. New York and New Jersey had an Interstate Sanitation Commission that dealt with air pollution. But in all cases, negotiations of the rules were understandably difficult. No state wanted to pay another for costs its citizens might impose on downstream users. And it was not in the interest of a state to adopt rules that pushed employers to seek lower cost locations in regions with abundant environmental quality. Competition among the states for an improved environment, income, and other important features of life tended to balance opposing forces. Since local citizens bore the costs and enjoyed the benefits of environmental control, they were better positioned to balance the benefits and costs.

The absence of federal jurisdiction and federal money forced people in states and cities to deal directly with the problem of environmental scarcity. They had no other choice. As a result, those closest to the problem and most sensitive to the costs resulting from their actions found innovative ways to deal with the problem. Instead of uniform rules, which are clearly simpler to enforce, local bodies could tailor controls to meet local conditions. Instead of relying on the existence of technology as an indication that the environment was improving, citizens looked at the air and water. Still, the problem of interstate competition and differential competitive costs plagued state and local politicians, just as it did the firms in their jurisdictions.

While movement of people and plants to locations having more of the scarce resource could have been the socially beneficial action, the cost of such changes created political demand for a national regulatory cartel. Federal regulation at least offered the prospect for improving environmental quality while maintaining populations in their current locations.

Social learning about pollution control was occurring in the pre-federal period and meaningful steps were taken to manage environmental quality, but at the same time, the nature of the pollution problem was changing. Murray Stein describes some of the changes and notes that, "At the turn of the century, 950 communities in the United States had provided sewers serving 24.5 million persons. Sixty communities provided some kind of sewage treatment for one million persons and the remainder discharged their wastes untreated. In 1900 the municipal wastes reaching streams had a pollution effect to the raw untreated sewage from a population of 24 million."[26]

Stein further notes that in 1900 pollution from industrial organic wastes had a population equivalent of 15 million persons. Handling the growing level of municipal wastes was the chief problem, which was strictly financial, not technical. The Great Depression simply made the problem worse. City and county governments were often bankrupt. But the New Deal pump priming programs came to the rescue. Until World War II, significant construction of treatment facilities occurred, and progress was made in the reduction of the discharge of raw sewage into streams.

The character of the pollution problem changed again in the post-World War II period. Industrial wastes were less frequently biodegradable and more often complex organic chemicals and heavy metals that could not be assimilated easily or handled by conventional sewage treatment plants. Between 1928 and 1958 the production of plastics grew from 20 million pounds annually to 4 billion pounds. Synthetic rubber production rose from zero to 2 billion pounds a year, and detergents from practically none to 1.3 billion pounds annually. The complex wastes associated with those products were joined by those from the production of nylon, new insecticides, and new organic drugs. The technical nature of pollution changed, as did the technologies for treating wastes. Pollution and pollution control became a more common feature of life. But nothing in the technical nature of the problem indicated that regulation could be better designed and enforced at the federal level.

CITIZEN INFLUENCE OF PRE-FEDERAL REGULATION

The argument that local citizens would be more sensitive to regulatory outcomes and expenditures in their own regions is fundamentally an empirical question, one that involves understandable conflicts about jobs, industrial growth, and the protection of the environment. What might the evidence say about these trade-offs?

One study of the pre-federal period sought to answer those questions in the context of state actions to control air pollution.[27] That study argues that all individuals in a political setting attempt to influence outcomes, but at the same time, there are conflicting goals and visions. Some people are more worried about jobs. Others are more concerned about maintaining the value of their land and homes.

Using data on the expenditures by states to regulate air pollution in 1967, the study set up a statistical experiment to determine the relationship between those expenditures across the fifty states and variables that accounted for the number of

workers employed in industries that typically were heavy dischargers of wastes, the total money income earned from real
property in the state, and the share of the work force unionized.
It was argued that local citizens would agree to spend relatively less where jobs were more threatened, and more where income from real property was larger. It was also expected that
organized labor would be influential in demanding more pollution control, after accounting for possible employment effects.

The results of the study showed that state expenditures on
pollution regulation could be largely explained by the variables just mentioned. Income from real property is strongly related to pollution control expenditures. Higher incomes
from real property are associated with larger state expenditures to control air pollution. Employment in polluting
industries is negatively related. The threat of job losses
from stringent air pollution regulation appears to have
a strong political influence. The effect of unions is much
weaker, although the influence appears to be positive.

The pre-federal study put forward the argument that local
citizens would have greater incentives for affecting the regulation of their local environments than people from some remote
location. It follows that regulatory outcomes would more accurately reflect the values of the people in the local setting.

There was a follow-up study that examined the pre- and post-
federal periods of air pollution control to determine the extent
to which local influence changed, if at all.[28] That study again
examined expenditures on air pollution regulation at the state
and local levels across the fifty states and did so for 1972, 1976,
and 1979. The underlying premise of the study argued that the
shift of regulation to the federal level from the state and local
jurisdictions altered the political strength of the various groups
that sought to influence outcomes.

Local citizens concerned about their natural environment—the owners of real property—were in a weaker position to lobby Congress than previously. National environmental groups, who generally were more concerned about
national parks and landmarks than a particular neighborhood in Cleveland, Ohio, gained strength. It was more costly
for those groups to lobby fifty state governments than one

federal government. At the same time, national labor unions gained.

The follow-up study also sought to determine if the older industrialized regions of the country, which were also the most polluted, systematically spent more or less on air pollution control than the newer regions. There was also a public health argument included in the study to determine if air pollution control efforts were more intensive where population was greater.

The results of the study were interesting for several reasons. First, the balance of political power did change. The interests of local property owners were swamped by other interests. Income from real property, proxied by the value of real property in this case, was no longer related to expenditures on air pollution control. Expenditures were higher for states with larger amounts of federal land located in their boundaries. The employment effect continued to influence expenditures negatively. Where unemployment risk was higher, pollution regulation was lower. The Frostbelt states spent no more or less on pollution control than the remaining states, after considering the influence of the other factors in the study. Once again, the union variable was not related to regulatory expenditures.

Taken together, the studies tell us that political influence matters in pollution control, and that it matters differently when the federal government attempts to regulate local environmental quality. The evidence suggests that nationally organized groups had more to gain from federal regulation than from state regulation and that the dirtier regions of the country made no greater effort to clean their environments than did the less industrialized regions.

The last point also suggests that pressure was placed on the cleaner regions to do more than they would have done otherwise. That is, the older industrialized regions could preserve their industrial position if somehow higher standards were imposed on the newly developing regions of the country.

SUMMARY

America's pre-federal experience with environmental regulation is as diverse as the country's population and geographic regions. Almost a century longer than the federal period, it was a time of experimentation with and development of ways to control polluter actions. The approaches taken by the various states and communities reflected environmental scarcity and trade-offs between economic opportunity and environmental quality. Common law remedies and property rights concepts were the means for resolving environmental problems for a major period of time. Instead of uniformity, there was rich diversity. Common law judges reflected on commonly held community values and rendered their decisions.

As pollution problems expanded across political jurisdictions and notions of public nuisance expanded, cities, counties, states, and then regions took action to write rules of conduct and to reach agreements on how the rules would be enforced. Ordinances, statutes, and compacts replaced common law courts and customs as the principle institutions for regulating the environment. Even then, diversity was the hallmark. Different states had different rules and approaches for controlling pollution, as did smaller political jurisdictions within states.

The stories about the pre-federal period contain strong special interest group influence. Environmental organizations form early and in some cases are supported by commercial and industrial interests. Exemptions and special treatment of particular groups are found throughout the period. But while economic forces were converted to political pressure to achieve specific goals, which were frequently clothed in public interest arguments, there was always competition. Cities, counties, and states could not act unilaterally in extreme ways. People and industry could move to other locations.

Empirical research that examines a part of the pre-federal experience and then compares the pre- and post-federal periods indicates the outcomes obtained by the same influences were different in the two periods. The research suggests that the shift of environmental control to the federal government carried with it higher payoffs for some interest groups, lower returns for others. We turn next to an examination of the federal experience.

NOTES

1. See Aaron Wildavsky, *Searching for Safety* (Bowling Green, Ohio: Social Philosophy and Policy Center, 1988), 18–25.

2. Joel A. Tarr, "Urban Pollution—Many Years Ago," *American Heritage*, vol. 22 (October 1971), 65.

3. *Calendar of the Patent Rolls*, 35 Edward 1, A.D. 1301–1307 (Leichtenstein: Kraus Reprint, 1971), 549.

4. *Ibid.*

5. See, for example, Julian C. Juergensmeyer, "Control of Air Pollution through the Assertion of Private Rights," *Duke Law Journal* (1967), 1126–44; Lawrence W. Pollack, "Legal Boundaries of Air Pollution Control—State and Local Legislative Purpose and Techniques," in Clark C. Havinghurst, ed., *Air Pollution Control* (New York: Oceana Publications, Inc., 1969); Harold W. Kennedy, "The Legal Aspects of Air Pollution Control with Particular Reference to the County of Los Angeles," *Southern California Law Review*, vol. 27 (1954), 373–414; Harold W. Kennedy and Andrew C. Porter, "Air Pollution: Its Control and Abatement," *Vanderbilt Law Review*, vol. 8 (1955), 854–77; Thomas A. Cowan, "Air Pollution Control in New Jersey," *Rutgers Law Review*, vol. 9 (1955), 609–33; Jeffrey Fromson, "A History of Federal Air Pollution Control," *Environmental Law Review—1970*, ed. H. Floyd Sherrod, Jr. (Albany, N.Y.: Sage Hill Publishers, Inc., 1970); James E. Krier, *Environmental Law and Policy* (Indianapolis: The Bobbs-Merrill Company, Inc., 1971).

6. See Fromson, "Federal Air Pollution Control," 125.

7. 113 Tenn. 331, 83 S.W. 658 (1904).

8. Victor J. Yannacone, Jr. and Bernard Cohen, *Environmental Rights and Remedies*, vol. 1 (Rochester, N.Y.: The Lawyers Co-Operative Publishing Company, 1972).

9. Kennedy and Porter, "Air Pollution: Its Control and Abatement," 859–60.

10. Krier, *Environmental Law and Policy*, 79.

11. F.E. Shuman, "Pittsburgh—'Smokeless City,'" *National Municipal Review*, vol. 39 (November 1950), 489–93.

12. See "Smog—Can Legislation Clear the Air?" *Stanford Law Review*, vol. 1 (April 1949), 452–62.

13. "Air Pollution Control," Information Report No. 20, *Planning Advisory Service* (American Society of Planning Officials, Nov. 1950), 1.

14. See Kennedy and Porter, "Air Pollution," 866–68.

15. F.E. Shuman, "Pittsburgh—'Smokeless City,' " 506.

16. For more on this, see, George T. Downey, *The Significance of Government Policies and Attitudes in Water Pollution Control: A Case Study of the Merrimack River Valley*, a dissertation for Clark University (Ann Arbor, Mich.: University Microfilms, 1969). The discussion here is also summarized in M.T. Maloney and Bruce Yandle, "Building Markets for Tradable Pollution Rights," Terry L. Anderson, ed., *Water Rights* (San Francisco: Pacific Institute for Public Policy Research, 1983), 283–320, esp. 299–300. A special note of appreciation is due Mike Maloney for an extended exchange of ideas and joint research efforts reflected in this chapter.

17. *Ibid.*, 125.

18. *Ibid.*, 143.

19. Kennedy and Porter, "Air Pollution," 871.

20. Pollack, "Legal Boundaries of Air Pollution Control," 145.

21. Norrell, Todd, and Alexander W. Bell, "Air Pollution Control in Texas," *Environmental Law Review—1970*, H. Floyd Sherrod, ed. (Albany, N.Y.: Sage Hill Publishers, Inc., 1970).

22. *Ibid.*, 246.

23. This discussion is based on Edward J. Cleary, *The Oransco Story*, Resources for the Future (Baltimore: The Johns Hopkins Press, 1967).

24. *Ibid.*, 42–43.

25. See Harvey Lieber, *Federalism and Clean Water*, (Lexington, Mass.: Lexington Books, 1975), 151–52.

26. Murray Stein, "Problems and Programs in Water Pollution," *Natural Resources Journal*, vol. 2, no. 3 (December 1962), 395–96.

27. See Bruce Yandle, "Economic Agents and the Level of Pollution Control," *Public Choice*, vol. 40, no. 1 (1983), 105–9.

28. Robert Quinn and Bruce Yandle, "Expenditures on Air Pollution Control Under Federal Regulation," *Review of Regional Studies*, vol. 16, no. 1 (Winter 1986), 11–16.

4

The Rise of the Federal Regulator

THE TRANSITION

Even though major pollution control institutions were in place in many state and local governments at the time, many writers identify 1945–1948 as the period marking the beginning of America's *national* concern over air pollution.[1] It was in 1945 that heavy smog in Los Angeles was viewed with public alarm. In 1948 several hundred people suffered respiratory difficulties attributed to air pollution in Denora, Pennsylvania, an event which brought national press coverage.

In terms of the environmental saga, the period might be labeled a time of transition, a time when the status of air quality was changing from a state and locally managed common-access resource to public property managed by the federal government where the political limits of environmental control would change. In a real sense, the federal government was at the threshold of defining federal property rights to the nation's air mantle. What previously had been a kind of competitive regulation marked by flexibility and experimentation at the state level was on the way to becoming hard and fast regulation by a monopolistic regulator that would have no competition.

As concern increased over the new form of air pollution—smog—and as scientists began to discover the causes and sources of that problem and other forms of air pollution, governments at every level received additional pressure to do something about the problem. Sometimes the pressure came from rather remote quarters and for unexpected reasons. The Los Angeles smog is a case in point.[2]

The systematic appearance of the yellowish brown cloud over Los Angeles no doubt distressed many local citizens, who voiced their concerns to elected officials. But one set of complaints that arrived could not be overlooked. Investment bankers in faraway Switzerland and insurance companies in Pennsylvania and Connecticut communicated in clear terms that something had to be done to protect the city's assets and tax base.

The bankers held Los Angeles bonds that had been issued to fund the construction of major city buildings. The insurance companies were holders of city debt and issuers of insurance. The economic message was imperative. The city was instructed to reduce the pollution or suffer the financial consequences. The bond holders threatened to demand payment on the bonds. The insurance companies questioned the ability of the city to pay for its insurance. Los Angeles took immediate steps to deal with smog.

As concern about air pollution spread across the nation, eyes turned toward smokestacks, and attention was fastened on plants and their stationary sources of pollution. Later, it was learned that mobile, not stationary, sources were the chief source of the new problem.

The property rights transition began nationally when the 1955 Air Pollution Control Act was passed, with a small budget of $5 million to support five years' activity. The law provided funding through the Department of Health, Education, and Welfare for research and development of control approaches.[3] Policies to deal with the pollution problem were still left for the states to determine.

Another bill was passed in 1962 authorizing investigations and hearings on interstate air pollution problems. Other investigative acts were passed, but it was not until 1967 and the passage of the Air Quality Act that federal management of the air mantle began to take form. Until then, Congress strongly opposed setting national air pollution standards, although action had been taken to study them.

SENATOR MUSKIE AND CLEAN AIR

The Air Quality Act of 1967 was drafted by the Senate Subcommittee on Air and Water Pollution, chaired by Senator Edmund Muskie of Maine.[4] On his way to becoming the vice presidential candidate in the 1968 election, the senator had spoken at the Earth Day rally in the late 1960s and was currying the favor of the environmentalists. Unfortunately for him, the legislation from his committee did not go far enough.

The 1967 act did not address stationary sources of pollution nor did it provide a system of national standards. Instead, the emphasis was on a regional approach to air pollution control, something akin to the approaches that had been taken by the more industrialized states. The legislation allowed for groups of affected people to register their individual preferences in determining different pollution control standards. Regional groups could establish rules reflecting their preferences, and the federal government would provide enforcement.

Where air pollution affected more than one state, conferences would be called by the Secretary of HEW to resolve the problem. A criteria document based on the conference would then be issued, and the states would have ninety days to deal with the order. However, even then the states were not required to specify pollution control methods. They could announce performance standards, goals for air quality to be achieved in a set time. Enforcement was the next issue.

Voters across America had not seen fit to pass laws that allowed regulators to enter plants, subpoena documents, or severely penalize firms that might be a major source of pollution.

In a word, the 1967 act had no teeth. The underlying theory of group action and performance standards sparkled with beneficial logic, but there was no mechanism for enforcing agreements once they were reached.

During the experience with the 1967 legislation, only one interstate action—one involving Union Carbide—appears to have been effectively resolved through federal guidance.[5] Indeed, through early 1970, not one criteria document was issued. Even so, much was learned about the difficulties of forcing control actions on state populations that did not appear to want them.

The pre-1970 air pollution legislation can be described generously as an effort to identify more precisely the nature of the problem, its boundaries, and the steps that might be taken to deal with it. Another view suggests several other forces were at work. First, the pollution problem was fully understood at the local level, but federal revenues could be obtained by shifting the problem to the federal level. Second, firms with national operations were frustrated by the quiltlike pattern of state regulations they faced and desired uniformity. They also saw an opportunity to lobby one legislature for beneficial rules instead of having to work the halls of fifty state legislatures.

Third, the environmental organizations forming at the time were national in scope and offered significant political strength to politicians that sought to design federal rules to their liking. The first view of the period sparkles with public interest logic. The second view is sprinkled with special interest logic.

In terms of the evolution of federal legislation, the 1955–1963 legislations focused on the nature of the problem and avoided regulation. As John Bonine describes that legislation, "The House Committee stressed: The bill does not propose an exercise of police power by the Federal Government, and no provisions in it invade the sovereignty of states, counties, or cities. There is no attempt to impose standards of purity."[6]

The 1963 Clean Air Act continued this focus, though some attention was devoted to the development of technologies for controlling air pollution. Again, John Bonine comments, "In one respect, the 1963 Act gave the Federal Government a role in abating pollution for the first time. Although it was not empowered to promulgate emission standards or regulations, the Federal Government was authorized to deal with interstate air pollution problems on an *ad hoc* basis."[7]

Though disavowed by legislators when debating the earlier legislation, federal rules were on the way. The Air Quality Act of 1967 put the finishing touches on the era when research and development was the primary focus.

The growing environmental movement was more than effective politicians could ignore. When crowds surged in the streets, politicians had an opportunity to respond to their concerns and gain votes. If the actions the politicians proposed failed to deliver the promised goods, a day of reckoning would come. Senator Muskie had learned this the hard way. He had sworn allegiance to the environmental movement but had not delivered the tough legislation that group demanded. Worse yet, he became the target of an attack by a Nader organization for being soft on polluters. As a potential candidate for the presidency in 1972, Muskie was compelled to react to the criticism.

Writing about this crucial period in the development of the national blueprint for controlling air pollution, Alfred Marcus notes that Muskie had favored a regional approach to the problem before the Nader-led attack.[8] After that, the senator changed his position and led the 1970 effort to legislate national uniform air quality standards. The Clean Air Act of 1970 was unanimously supported by the Senate, passed by a 371–1 vote in the House, and was signed by President Nixon.

TECHNOLOGY AS A BASIS FOR REGULATION

The Clean Air Act of 1970 (CAA) was heralded by many as marking a major shift in the means for securing the goals announced in the 1967 act. Vividly optimistic comments were made by the Council on Environmental Quality in its 1971 report.[9] Technology-based standards coupled to the national standards formed the linchpin of the new system. While the council talked about economic incentives elsewhere in the report, the relevant section extolling the virtues of command and control said, "The Federal quality program changed dramatically when the Clean Air Amendments became law. They embody recommendations contained in the President's 1970 Message on the Environment and proposed significant control for new pollution sources and for all facilities emitting hazardous substances. It also established a framework for the States to set emission standards for existing sources in order to achieve national air quality standards."[10]

The CAA contained the needed muscle for the new federal regulator—EPA—and mandated specific requirements for setting national ambient air quality standards (NAAQS) to be managed through EPA-approved state plans. Along with the details describing the federal takeover of state functions were deadlines for attaining the standards. Significantly, the approach served to identify boundaries to new public property rights to be secured and managed by the federal government (and therefore private property rights to existing polluters who operated legally within the standards). Although that step was not viewed initially as being significant, the means for delivering the new public property was. Congress broke with the past practice of regulating to achieve some targeted ambient level of air quality and seized technology, the machinery for cleaning emissions at each source, as the policy instrument for its enforcement operations.

Once identified by EPA, a specific technology, such as "best available control technology" (BACT) was to be the basis of enforceable contracts with each noncomplying polluter included by states in their EPA-approved State Implementation Plan (SIP), the final contract between the states and the federal government. Every state was to have an EPA-approved plan, which was to demonstrate an explicit approach for achieving the national standards. Each major source of pollution was to be listed in the plan, along with a process for monitoring and approving all new construction and expansions of existing plants that might be built in a given state. States that failed to develop an approved plan were to have their control programs run by EPA. A regulatory cartel was formed—one that set uniform rules for all members and contained sanctions for those who cheated on the system.

THE EPA-MANAGED CARTEL

The shift from performance standards to technology-based rules for new and modified stationary sources of emissions

was an effective monopolizing device for EPA. The requirement promised uniformity and skirted the problem of monitoring emissions that had been so difficult in the pre-1970 period.
The public property secured by Congress and managed by EPA
was ostensibly certain qualitative aspects of the air mantle.

Those supporting the federal move saw visions of numerous monitoring stations located across the United States that
would identify the pre- and post-control levels of emissions and
assure the delivery of cleaner air. But, as it turned out, air
quality was not monitored carefully, neither before nor after
controls were applied.

The EPA process for defining control technologies and emission guidelines placed important emphasis on industry data.
Before preparing final rules for an industry, EPA would complete a thorough industry study, acquiring data that would nor-
mally be used by an industrial planner. Data on every major
plant in an industry would be gathered, and a financial impact
analysis completed.

Plants in the industry would be placed into size categories:
small, medium, and large. Simulations would then be run to
observe the effects of alternative control strategies. The expected plant closings, price increases, and output effects would
then be estimated. During the completion of a study, industry members and others would have access to the underlying
data, although efforts were made to disguise sensitive firm-
level data. Nonetheless, the study process itself increased the
demand for industry-wide cooperation and provided composite
information on cost and output that previously was barred by
antitrust statutes.

Once EPA rules were implemented, installation of machinery and the construction of new plants were monitored, for that
was the nexus of control. Sources lacking the appropriate control technologies had to prove their innocence, without regard
to the quality of the air before and after the plant's operations
began. Environmental quality ceased to be the goal of the law;
installing and operating machinery became the focus.

Technology was the object of contracts between environmental control authorities and the owners of plants. When seeking
to prove guilt of environmental trespass—the unauthorized

use of the new public property—proof boiled down to the existence and operation of the specified machinery. The complex monitoring problem was solved once and for all, even though air quality might or might not be improved.

DIFFERENTIAL ENFORCEMENT OF THE LAW

Technology-based environmental control offered a further possibility to existing firms and, in some sense, contained the seeds of monopoly power for affected industries. To the extent that existing firms could postpone or avoid enforcement actions while new firms could not, an effective barrier to entry was erected. If the standards were set at impossible attainment levels, existing firms had little fear the rules would be enforced. The political machinery just couldn't shut down an entire industry for failing to meet impossible standards. At the same time, the impossible standards might be applied to new firms that lacked the political muscle to gain their relaxation. Unborn firms have little political clout. The new rules strengthened the status quo, which meant the continuation of polluting plants.

Describing the situation after reviewing the impossible enforcement situation posed by the technology-based standards, and the implicit advantage given existing firms, Freeman and Haveman wrote, "(T)here is the further consideration that, should the rules actually be enforced, the cost would be enormous. Given existing technology and its foreseeable developments attainment of the best available technology . . . will be prohibitively expensive."[11]

Anderson and Kneese, commenting on the ease with which existing firms could escape compliance, add, "(W)here its abatement options are expensive and of doubtful reliability, a firm can reasonably expect to make a convincing case in court about the infeasibility or unreasonableness of the (EPA's) emission requirements. At the very least, it can avoid presenting a case so flimsy a judge will react punitively."[12]

The realities of the compliance problem surfaced when electric utilities attempted to switch to low sulfur fuels to meet EPA's national standard. Public utility managers had resisted installing stack scrubbers to remove sulfur oxides partly because of regulatory lag in gaining approval for the additional capital in their rate bases. Low sulfur fuel was a simpler alternative, since fuel costs were automatically approved by public utility regulators. A switch to gas and oil was encouraged by the environmental regulators.[13]

When the Arab embargo hit and energy replaced the environment as a number one national concern, the utilities had a new problem. Their supplies of low sulfur gas and oil were drying up, leaving higher sulfur coal and costly scrubbers as the only alternative. By that time, it was impossible to change control strategies, install scrubbers, and achieve the EPA air quality deadline of June 1975.

The public utilities were caught between the Emergency Energy Act, which called for conversion to coal, and EPA, which required emission limitations on sulfur dioxide. But EPA was caught also, since the agency had not forced the installation of the scrubbers. The solution, which was most favorable to existing generating plants, came in a series of EPA-approved variances that postponed the 1975 deadline. Those allowed existing utilities to continue lower-cost production of electricity and highlighted the difficulties that emerged when environmental quality faced competition from another national problem.

GETTING MONOPOLY POWER THROUGH REGULATION

The differential enforcement of standards across industries and between new and old plants illustrates how competitive advantage can be gained from regulation and the variances associated with them. Concern about the problem and a prediction regarding political pressures to come from it were expressed early in the 1971 *Economic Report of the President*: "New rules for the use of the environment are bound to affect competitive relationships. As industries are forced to bear the costs of using the environment, those who have high costs will lose part of their markets to those with lower costs of using the environment. Inevitably, there will be pressures for Government action to prevent this reallocation of production."[14]

Recalling that federal regulation had been supported because of the problems faced when national firms had to deal with fifty different state regulations, it is interesting that federal regulation produced a similar problem. There was an important difference, however, at least insofar as the federal politicians might be concerned. Under the federal regime, the political pressures would come to bear in Washington. That meant that lobbying energies would not be dissipated across fifty states. The concentration of control brought with it a concentration of political power and the associated gains.

There is no clear evidence that industrial firms fought for higher new source standards that would limit the entry of new competition. But they did not have to. Environmentalists did the job for them. The industrialists and environmentalists were like bootleggers and Baptists in a state referendum over selling alcoholic beverages on Sunday. The Baptists take the high ground and put forth moral arguments about the evils of alcohol. They monitor the law enforcement officers and make certain that corner liquor stores close on Sunday, bringing legal action when necessary. Meanwhile the bootleggers enjoy an expanded market where entry is barred by Baptist action.

The significant role played by environmentalists in securing entry limiting barriers was buttressed by legislation in the 1970 CAA that ushered in the day of related citizens' suits.[15] The new law deputized all citizens and gave them an incentive to enforce whatever rules EPA might promulgate. Commenting on the additional enforcement action, the Council on Environmental Quality stated, "One of the most striking and significant developments in environmental law is the right of citizens to take to court Federal agency actions affecting the environment. NEPA (the National Environment Policy Act) and other laws require agencies to consider the environment in their actions. And citizens are now initiating lawsuits when they believe an agency has failed to do that."[16]

The new deputies and environmental activists served as enforcers of the new public property defined by the federal regulator. Part of the new property rights were endowed to the public, but there was also property endowed to existing polluters. So long as current polluters abided by the rules, they could be assured of limited encroachment on their sites. The protection they enjoyed added value to scarcer industrial locations and also raised the cost of all newly entering competitors.

ENCOUNTERS WITH BROKEN DEADLINES

June 30, 1975, marked an important date in the regulation of air quality. That was the date for all air quality regions to meet the national air quality standards. Those that could not were labeled nonattainment areas, which triggered a new set of sanctions. There were many regions that failed to meet the deadline, 102 out of 247.[17] The nonattainment designation placed restrictions on future growth in that no new major source of air pollution could enter the areas, even if the new source met the most stringent pollution control standards. While the limitation placed a burden on the dirtier regions, it simultaneously distributed benefits to regions that were in compliance. Locations where development could occur became more valuable.

The arrival of the deadline was also important for existing plants in the dirtier regions. The nonattainment label limited the entry of new competition to their specific areas with much greater precision than did the earlier new source performance standards. In the previous period, new entry was only limited by the higher cost controls required of new sources. In the nonattainment period, entry was barred. The effect on property rights to pollute are obvious. Their property became more valuable.

With entry barred, the existing sources could argue logically and with much more enthusiasm for cost-effective regulatory rules. Operators of existing plants in nonattainment regions could go for increased profits without the fear that higher profits would attract new competitive entry. The passage of June

30, 1975, solidified the ownership of pollution rights to existing firms and offered smoother avenues for seeking more efficient regulation, lower costs, and higher profits.

THE CHEVRON CASE

A prime example of emerging property rights to environmental use occurred in California in 1974.[18] Looking back, it might have been expected. From the outset of the enforcement of regulations spawned by the 1970 CAA, California was destined to be a nonattainment region for hydrocarbon and sulfur dioxide emissions. Initially, this meant that plant expansions could be built so long as stringent control technologies were applied. The strict controls implied that reasonable progress was underway to attainment. But that was not enough. By 1974 the handwriting was on the wall. California officials realized that attainment was an impossible goal. A standard of no new emissions was adopted. Even with the strictest controls, state-of-the-art design could not meet the zero standard. Practically speaking, the decision meant no new industrial growth.

At the time, Chevron USA, a subsidiary of Standard Oil of California, had plans to construct a new refinery at Richmond, California. As the firm's second largest refinery, the new unit was intended to replace two small older units. When completed, the new refinery would employ 2,500 workers and have a capacity of 315,000 barrels of refined oil daily, compared with the combined capacity of 90,000 barrels daily from the two older plants.

To gain construction permits for the new plant, Chevron officials agreed to shut down the two older plants when the new one came on line. The proposed strategy sparkled with regulatory logic. By making the trade, the air pollution control authorities could satisfy several popular objectives while meeting their own requirement for zero new pollution. The shutdown of the older facilities would reduce emissions by more than the amount added by the new plant. Employment opportunities would expand, more refined oil would be produced, and the environment would be improved. The Bay Area

Pollution Control District accepted the deal, taking an action that implicitly assigned pollution property rights to Chevron's previous level of emissions.

Upon completion of the new plant, however, Chevron continued to operate the older plants. Finally, in November 1977, California Standard was instructed to shut down the new plant, since the firm had failed to live up to its agreement with the authorities. Chevron challenged the order, pointing out that the total emissions from the entire complex of plants—new and old—was less than the 1974 level. Obviously, some modification of processes or changes in output levels must have occurred in the older facilities. The firm went on to argue that regulations allowed them to operate the new facilities if the total modified facility showed no net increase. Chevron attempted to protect the implicit property rights.

Out of controversies such as this came the seeds of a new approach to air pollution control. Transferable pollution rights were emerging. If the mechanism received the enforcement authority's blessing, firms would have the opportunity to minimize cost within the limits of some total level of allowable emissions. Plants could be reconstructed, and new plant capacity could be added so long as some total amount of pollution was maintained. That flexibility would allow local economies to respond to changes in demand for products and services, while at the same time preserving some targeted level of environmental quality. In that sense, a net social gain lay waiting for approval of the new mechanism.

THE EMERGENCE OF TRADEABLE EMISSION RIGHTS

What was to be hailed as EPA's most innovative policy for dealing with air pollution since the passage of the 1970 CAA was announced by John R. Quarles, EPA Deputy Administrator, in a November 1976 speech in California.[19] The speech was interesting for many reasons. Quarles placed special emphasis on the problem caused by new emission sources and reaffirmed the policy of placing stricter controls on them. Looked at in a different light, Quarles assured existing polluters that competition for their scarce sites would be blocked by EPA. He noted that:

(Congress) really had no more idea than we (EPA) did just how serious the problem of growth would turn out. To illustrate the dimensions of the problem, let me turn to the impact of projected new plants on air pollution alone. National emissions from stationary sources of hydrocarbons will almost double by 1990 if additional controls are not imposed on new sources of hydrocarbons. The picture for particulates is almost as gloomy. Without additional controls on new stationary sources, emissions are expected to increase by over 50 percent by 1990. Without reductions in emissions from new facilities, we are in danger of falling back to conditions even worse than those which existed before we started.[20]

Opportunity cost of environmental quality was now being recognized. The regulators and those who bore the burden of the search for cleaner air were coming face-to-face with the trade-offs, and the outlook was not too pleasant.

In the face of this, Quarles offered a partial solution for California and other regions that were destined to hit the regulatory wall. It was a property rights solution that paralleled the Chevron argument. The policy, which became known as EPA's Offset Policy, was that after applying the strictest control at each source of emissions, a new major facility could enter a nonattainment area like California if it could obtain emission reductions for the same pollutant from existing polluters and in a sufficient amount to more than offset the pollution added by the new source.[21]

As might be expected, support for the idea was far short of unanimous. Environmentalists were immediately suspicious. They tended to view the mechanism as just another way to placate industries that constantly cried wolf about the impossibility of reducing pollution. Offsets would simply make it easier to postpone the day of reckoning that had to come. Industrialists wondered how on earth they would ever find sufficient offsets to construct a major plant. The logic of the idea might have appeal, but making a market was something else.

The new offset policy represented a conceptual crossing of a property rights threshold. For fences to be erected, progress had to be made in the identification, measurement, and enforcement of air pollution emissions. Then, for trades to be allowed, a baseline had to be established. The pollution property of dry cleaners had to be distinguishable from the similar property of electric generators. If that became known, a new asset would emerge on the balance sheets of polluters. The existing polluters would be able to capitalize the value of their existing positions. Newly entering firms would have to buy their way into the nonattainment regions.

The implied property rights regime offered a solution to EPA's no-growth policies, but while capitalizing the value of pollution rights for existing firms, opened the door for competition. Of course, new competition for existing oil refineries would have to buy the right to emit hydrocarbons, but not from existing refineries. There were many other sources of hydrocarbon emissions, including dry cleaners. The new firm would shop for rights, just as it would shop for land to use in constructing plants. Emissions would be bought from the lowest bidder.

As it turned out, the offset policy created far more excitement among economists and policy analysts, who loved the underlying economic logic but have hardly any political influence, than among industrialists and regulators, who make the political machinery hum. The bureaucratic complexities associated with approving just one offset transaction formed a high hurdle. Added to that were horrendous uncertainties regarding just what was being bought, how the transfer would be made, and how the new rights would be protected. The question of political uncertainty was even worse. How would a buyer of emission rights know that Congress would continue to allow the rule to exist, not change the definition of attainment and nonattainment, and by taking such actions confiscate the new property in one fell swoop of the pen?

As troublesome as these questions might be, even more difficult problems developed when some of the first offset transactions were attempted.[22] The Standard Oil of Ohio (SOHIO) case illustrates some of the difficulties. In 1978 SOHIO had been trying for three years to gain the needed environmental permits to build a crude oil unloading facility near Long Beach, California. The firm had access to a transcontinental pipeline at that location, had oil coming from the Alaskan North Slope, and needed a way to move the oil to the lower forty-eight states.

In the wake of the 1974 Arab oil embargo, Congress had passed legislation prohibiting the export of American crude oil. Otherwise, SOHIO could have shipped crude to Japan, where it could have been refined and reshipped to the United States. SOHIO's only other alternative involved shipping the oil in super tankers around the tip of South America and bringing the oil to Galveston, Texas, where unloading facilities could handle the movement from there. Long Beach, California, was the more attractive possibility.

After delays in the attempts to get environmental permits, and knowing that unloading the crude oil would produce hydrocarbon emissions, SOHIO hit on the idea of buying an oil refinery in the Long Beach area, dismantling it, and using the emission reductions to offset what its new facility would add. There was more than a one-for-one offset available. The plot thickened.

The California pollution control authorities tightened the screw. They increased the offset ratio and instructed SOHIO to find more reductions. The firm contacted California Edison and signed an agreement to pay for the installation of improved pollution controls on that firm's emissions. SOHIO also negotiated with local dry cleaners and agreed to pay them to install more sophisticated pollution control devices on their plants. By then, the cost of the offsets had risen to $90 million.

Each time it appeared that SOHIO had made a deal, the control authorities increased the ratio, attempting to force the firm to clean even more air while delivering its oil. Finally, negotiations broke down. SOHIO altered its course of action and moved the oil by ship to Galveston. In the process, Long Beach lost air emission reductions, U.S. consumers paid more for oil, and Galveston gained hydrocarbon emissions.

The political economy of the incident is rather clear. Firms seeking offsets faced a moving target that could be manipulated in ways to extract the greatest possible payment from the buyer.

In California's case, the person in charge at the state level was also the campaign finance chairman for a governor who aspired to be president of the United States. Environmentalism was riding high, but the market for offsets was not.

Some of the other early transactions came easier. Volkswagen of America was allowed to build a plant in Pennsylvania when the state of Pennsylvania provided offsets by changing from petroleum-base to water-base asphalt for highway construction and repair. In that case, the politicians wanted the plant and faced pressure from a high unemployment region to get the plant operating. General Motors opened its Oklahoma City plant after obtaining offsets developed through the good offices of the city's Chamber of Commerce. Emissions were reduced by the operator of an oil distribution firm, which installed improved emission controls on storage tanks. Where the politics was right, offsets seemed to work. But where the political pressure groups favored command and control, the market crumbled.

It is worth noting that EPA's Offset Policy, which became a favorite showpiece of environmental economists, emerged from state action, not from Washington. The innovative ability of competitive regulation to produce improved regulation is observed. According to former EPA Assistant Administrator Charles Quarles, EPA officials were not attempting to find ways to minimize cost, organize efficient markets, or in any way appeal to theoretical logic of economics when offsets were embraced.[23] The administrators were simply trying to find a way out of an impossible situation.

California and other states were facing a no-growth situation. The nonattainment states were about to be in a box where draconian penalties would apply. First, no major industrial growth would be allowed. Then, the state would lose federal highway and urban transportation money. All of that was impossible politically. If EPA attempted to implement the enforcement tools given in its legislative mandate and growth in major states was actually stopped, the regulators' ability to stay in business would surely crumble in a showdown with Congress. Offsets and other forms

of control that used economic logic were a political neces-
sity.

THE EMERGING BUBBLE CONCEPT

The combination of normal economic growth and change, the
drift of technological improvements, and the constraint on environmental use was destined to bring more old plants to the
point where they would have to undertake major reconstruc-
tion. EPA rules allowed for modifications of equipment without confronting the strict new source pollution standards, up
to a point. But that point was reached when plants just had
to be rebuilt from scratch. The arrival of the time when old
and new plants had to face the stricter standards increased
the strength of the coalition lobbying for some way around
the costly standards. Old plants have constituents—their employees, suppliers, and elected officials. The yet-to-exist new
plants are much weaker politically. The added political force
of entrenched plants was welcomed to the battleground.

In 1977 EPA ruled that an existing plant could make modifications of the Chevron type described earlier and avoid new
source review, provided the plant management demonstrated
that no net additional emissions would result from the new facilities. The interpretation by EPA stretched the meaning of
certain words in the 1970 CAA as they had been applied and
interpreted in other decisions. Earlier, EPA had said each single machine and process in a single building had to be treated
as a pollution source. If proportional pollution reductions were
required, each and every machine would have to be controlled
accordingly.

The pivotal issue had to do with the meaning of the words
source and facility. If best available technology was to be applied to all new sources, and if a new source was any machine
that released emissions, EPA could not release that source
from meeting the regulatory requirements. However, if EPA
now revised its interpretation of the law, trouble was bound
to come from at least two places: The environmental organizations that were suspicious about any relaxation of standards

and other industrial firms that had been forced to meet the original interpretation of the law.

EPA's attempt to allow a plant to consider all sources together when reaching for an improvement in overall emission levels—something akin to the Chevron approach—was attacked by the combined forces of the Sierra Club and ASARCO, Inc., one of the oldest environmental organizations and one of the nation's largest copper smelters. ASARCO maintained the policy would have to be applied to new plants, if it was applied to old ones. The Sierra Club simply opposed any move that would allow more emissions to come from a single machine.

While EPA's effort made sense in terms of cost-effectiveness, the U.S. Court of Appeals simply read the law and interpreted it. The court ruled that "The Environmental Protection Agency's "bubble concept" of defining stationary sources for the purposes of compliance with Clean Air Act New Source Performance Standards violates the Act."[24] Though set back by the court ruling, EPA and some industry groups began to agitate for flexibility and cost-effective solutions to the control of air pollution.

The possibility of defining a conceptual bubble cast over a collection of emission sources and focusing on how much escaped into the environment instead of tinkering with each and every machine in a plant and hoping that total emissions would be reduced turned on the ability to measure emissions, monitor the environment, and enforce contracts across sources. The proof that emissions from one machine could be reduced while offsetting those from another machine in the same plant was what bothered the Sierra Club. Would firms hoodwink the regulators?

The Sierra Club was not alone with its concern. Polluters affected by the rules were also concerned. Lenient treatment of a polluter was all that it took to wipe out the value of hard-won pollution rights. The value of the right to use the environment would fall to zero, if uncontrolled pollution invaded protected territories. With enough deterioration, pressures for cleaner air would reach the point that standards would be tightened even further.

THE OVERLOOKED CLEAN AIR REGIONS

When the 1970 CAA and the regulations that followed it began to be translated into EPA-approved state plans for managing environmental use, firms seeking to expand operations and encountering strict controls naturally focused on alternative locations. Although the choices were limited by the EPA-induced regulatory cartel that had set uniform minimum air quality standards across the fifty states, there was a loophole worth considering. Some regions had air quality that exceeded the national standards, and the price of consuming the excess quality was effectively zero. In focusing on how to improve the dirty regions, Congress had overlooked an attractive escape mechanism for expansion-bound industries.

In some cases, the cleaner regions contained national parks or were located near such national treasures. In other cases, the cleaner regions simply lacked the population density and industry that ordinarily deteriorate environmental quality. Whatever the explanation, the clean regions offered an opportunity for firms to expand output. The regulatory cartel was threatened.[25]

Perhaps unwittingly, EPA was on the threshold of allowing competitive expansion of industries in the pristine regions. Since additional emissions in those locations would not interfere with the attainment of national air quality standards, the agency had little choice but to allow the invasion of the clean regions by industrial plants. But members of the Sierra Club thought otherwise. Once again, an environmental organization performed the task of protecting a regulatory cartel that limited the expansion of competition while simultaneously seeking to protect environmental quality. When on the verge of approving state plans that allowed expansion, EPA was sued by the Sierra Club. The action first led to a court injunction that prohibited EPA's approval of such plans. When the action was appealed to the Supreme Court by EPA, twenty states filed briefs supporting the lower court's ruling. After a split decision by the Court on June 11, 1973, the lower court's ruling was left to stand. The Court instructed EPA to develop regulations that assured that no significant deterioration of air quality would occur in the clean air regions. The Court also stipulated that the regulations would be final unless vetoed by Congress. Those regulations were published on December 4, 1974.[26]

The Court-ordered review by Congress was a crucial step in the story. Prior to the Court action, Congress had debated legislation to deal with the clean region problem. Western senators, who favored development and had clean air to spare, blocked the proposed amendments to the CAA. However, when time came to consider EPA's proposed rules, the Eastern senators, who sought to protect the economic positions of industries in their regions rose to meet the challenge. In a marvelously paradoxical move and in the name of protecting the citizens of the Western senators, politicians in the East protected themselves.[27]

EPA's 1974 regulations for the prevention of significant deterioration (PSD) specified a classification system for all regions having air quality above the national standard and identified allowable increments of certain air pollutants for each classification. Generally speaking, the 1974 regulations allowed for minor deterioration in areas designated CLASS I, moderate reductions in air quality in CLASS II regions, and deterioration closer to the national standard in CLASS III regions. In no case would air quality be allowed to fall to the level of the national standard.

With all the loopholes closed, EPA was on the way to completing the cartelization of the market. Each state regulator was now an important player in the regulatory scheme. Plans for dealing with existing industries and their expansions were in place, and the targeted level of air quality for every region in the United States had been defined.

IS ENVIRONMENTAL QUALITY REGULATION A UNICORN?

By 1976, EPA had experienced five frustrating years as regulator under the CAA of 1970. Much had been done on paper and in the courts, but little had been done to obtain the substantive results called for in the basic legislation. Aside from the sheer complexity of the regulatory task itself, there were other explanations offered for EPA's lack of success in achieving the environmental goals.

Stephen Breyer touched on several explanations.[28] First, in the pre-federal period, the states had set very general standards and used enforcement to custom tailor them to individual situations. There had been more flexibility in the system. EPA had gone about setting highly specific standards but was extremely slow in getting its rules published in final form. Quite naturally, polluters waited to see what the rules would be. It was risky to invest in pollution control equipment that might later fail to meet the regulator's standard. As a consequence, there were long periods where nothing happened.

Next, Breyer pointed out that it was difficult to know when a firm was actually in compliance. Monitoring of emissions was inadequate for the purpose and very little emphasis was placed on that activity by the regulator. Just getting out the specification standards seemed the challenge to be met, not improving the environment. In addition, the uncertainty of receiving a fine for noncompliance was quite large. If a violation was found, a firm could bargain for a reduced penalty or threaten to go to court. Quite often, the reluctant firm could prove that it was actually in compliance, since EPA had no data to prove otherwise. The firm also might argue successfully that the rules were unreasonable, or that more time was needed to meet them. In short, polluters had little to lose by waiting to comply and going to court if caught taking that posture. All along, of course, the polluters could operate in a competitive environment where new entrants faced the full regulatory screen. Those standing at the threshold could never argue that they were in compliance, nor could they argue on the basis of fact that the new source standards were unreasonable.

Federal air quality regulation was beginning to look more like a unicorn. There were elaborate descriptions of details and behavior, but no one could really admit to having seen the real process in full operation. And oddly enough, in some ways, there was no real pressure placed on Congress to publish a verifiable report card on progress. Instead, those interested in environmental quality constantly pushed for more rules, as if rules alone were the goal, not improvements in the environment.

Empirical Studies that Support the Unicorn Theory

Saying that the elaborate maze of controls was more mythical than real with regard to making progress toward meeting environmental goals certainly doesn't imply there were no real effects. Quite the contrary, federal air quality regulations were supported and opposed with real expenditures, because the rules themselves were exceedingly valuable to some and exceedingly costly to others. Two important pieces of research illustrate the point.

The first category of research focused on how the stricter standards for new plant and cleaner regions affected different regions of the country.[29] Forgetting about environmental quality, which is the presumed purpose of the regulation, the research asked other questions: Can one examine the voting behavior of politicians from the dirtier regions and observe systematic behavior that suggests they were simply attempting to thwart the exit of industrial jobs from their regions? Is there evidence that air quality control regulation affected the competitive positions of small versus large firms?

The work done on these two questions provides exceptionally strong support for both propositions. Examination of voting patterns for clean air legislation and amendments reveals the semblance of a special interest group that has as its purpose the control of industrial growth in ways that preserve the status quo of industrial states. Simply put, legislation intending to be tough on polluters is directed toward newer regions that offer less polluted locations for people and industry. The dirtier regions face less strict controls than the regions that have little or no industry.

Along with the regional effects came biases against smaller plants and firms. The capital intensive rules favored large firms and large plants, again supporting the status quo. At the margin, new firms and plants had to start with larger capital investments, which limited economic growth and improvement in national income.

The second category of research looked at air pollution regulation as a device to give monopoly power to existing firms.[30] Taking the approach that EPA was actually a cartel manager that served the interests of a coalition of environmentalists and industrialists who both wanted restrictions of pollution, this research asked one central question: Is there persuasive evidence that identifiable firms and industries actually gained profits when EPA tightened its control of air pollution?

The research focused on the copper industry, which faced severe challenges in reducing emissions of sulfur dioxide from smelters. A number of significant regulatory events were identified that marked the times when EPA and the courts tightened the standards to be met by the industry. The performance of a portfolio of copper company stocks relative to the market was then examined rigorously to determine if that portfolio increased in value at the time the restrictions were increased. The answer was affirmative. The research also examined a safety and health regulation enforced by the Occupational Safety and Health Administration (OSHA) in an effort to generalize the theory. Similar effects were found when OSHA tightened an industrial standard faced by the cotton processing industry. Firms that used more cotton gained more profits.

While none of these studies on the cartel effects of the Clean Air Act of 1970 and its amendments sought to determine the extent to which EPA's enforcement of the laws actually tended to reduce rather than improve air quality, that challenge was met in a later study of the electricity industry, a chief source of sulfur dioxide and particulate emissions.[31] The question here had to do with the differential standards faced when firms consider how long to operate an old plant. The firm can either repair and maintain an old facility and meet less strict pollution standards or build a new plant and have to face extremely costly new source performance standards. Obviously, one can imagine cases where a firm would choose to keep an old plant operating and continue to pollute by doing so.

The researchers focused on elements of the capital investment decision for the years 1957 through 1982 and modeled the effects of the 1970 CAA as it was enforced, modified, and amended. The results of the study show clearly that older plants operated for longer periods as the restrictions tightened. When the effects of this on emissions were estimated, the researchers found that emissions in the northeastern states in 1980 were 20 percent higher than they would have been in the absence of the new source performance standards. In other words, *the legislation had the effect of making the air dirtier than it would have been.* If federal environmental regulation was a unicorn, it was a dirty unicorn.

NOTES

1. For a discussion of this watershed period, see A. Myrick Freeman and Robert H. Haveman, "Clean Rhetoric and Dirty Water," in Alain C. Enthoven and A. Myrick Freeman, *Pollution, Resources, and the Environment* (New York: W.W. Norton and Company, Inc., 1973), 253–86; Allen Kneese and Charles L. Schultze, *Pollution, Prices and Public Policy,* (Washington: The Brookings Institution, 1975), 45–47; and Joseph Palomba, Jr., "Air Pollution Control," *The Annals,* vol. 444 (July 1979), 68–69.

2. This episode was reported by Saxe Dobrin, an official with a state air pollution control agency in Southern California, in remarks presented to a Manufacturing Chemists Association meeting in Washington, D.C., February 27–28, 1979.

3. A discussion of the early federal legislation is found in John E. Bonine, "The Evaluation of 'Technology Forcing' in the Clean Air Act," *Environment Reporter Monograph, No. 21,* vol. 6, no. 13 (July 25, 1975), 1–30; and Kneese and Schultze, *Pollution, Prices and Public Policy,* 30–50.

4. See also Alfred Marcus, "Environmental Protection Agency," James Q. Wilson, ed., *The Politics of Regulation* (New York: Basic Books, 1980), 267–303.

5. The case is discussed in Lawrence D. Hines, *Environmental Issues: Population, Pollution, Economics* (New York: W. W. Norton and Company, 1973), 280–82.

6. See Bonine, "Evaluation of 'Technology Forcing ' " 3.

7. See Bonine, "Evaluation of 'Technology Forcing ' " 3–4.

8. Marcus, "Environmental Protection Agency," 273.

9. See Council on Environmental Quality, *Environmental Quality*, the second annual report of the Council on Environmental Quality (Washington: Government Printing Office, August 1971), 8.

10. Ibid.

11. See Freeman and Haveman, "Clean Rhetoric and Dirty Water," 130–31.

12. Frederick R. Anderson, Allen V. Kneese, Phillip D. Reed, et al., *Environmental Improvement Through Economic Incentives* (Washington: Resources for the Future, 1977), 15.

13. Richard E. Ayers, "Enforcement of Air Pollution Controls on Stationary Sources Under the Clean Air Amendments of 1970," *Ecology Law Quarterly*, vol. 4, no. 3 (1975), 441–78.

14. *Economic Report of the President, 1971* (Washington: Government Printing Office, 1971), 12.

15. See Council on Environmental Quality, *Environmental Quality, 1971*, p. 122. A parallel action occurred for water pollution. (See U.S. Congress, Committee on Government Operations, 91st Congress, 2nd. Session, "Qui Tam Actions and the 1899 Refuse Act: Citizens Lawsuits Against Polluters of the Nation's Waterways," 1970.

16. Council on Environmental Quality, Ibid.

17. See Jack L. Landau, "Who Owns the Air? The Emission Offset Concept and Its Implications," *Environmental Law*, vol. 9, no. 3 (Spring 1979), 578. Another observer reported that 156 of 247 regions missed the deadline for at least one pollutant. (See Douglas Martin, "Curb on Construction Where Air Is Dirty Rankles Businessmen," *The Wall Street Journal*, May 4, 1977, pp. 1 and 32.

18. For various reports on the Chevron case, see "Agency Warns Unit of California Standard on Refinery Emissions," *The Wall Street Journal*, January 9, 1978, p. 25; *Air/Water Pollution Report*, December 5, 1977, vol. 15, no. 49, p. 481; January 16, 1978, vol. 16, no. 3, p. 28; March 20, 1978, vol. 16, no. 12, p. 111; and in "California Standard Unit Is Told to Close New Refinery by Pollution Control Panel," *The Wall Street Journal*, November 25, 1978.

19. See John R. Quarles, "To Grow or Not to Grow—That Is Not the Question," Fifth Annual International Pollution Engineering Congress (Anaheim, California, November 10, 1976).

20. Ibid., 2–3.

21. Further discussion of the mechanism is found in Landau, "Who Owns the Air," 578; Bruce Yandle, "The Emerging Market in Air Pollution Rights," *Regulation*, (July/August 1978), 21–29; and U.S.

Environmental Protection Agency, "Emission Offset Interpretive Ruling," *Federal Register*, vol. 44, no. 11 (January 16, 1979).

22. Yandle, "The Emerging Market in Air Pollution Rights," 21–29.

23. Conversation with Quarles, February 27, 1979.

24. See "Appeals Court Rejects EPA NSPS (New Source Performance Standards) Stationary Source Definition," *Environment Reporter* (February 10, 1978), 1569–73.

25. See Arthur C. Stern, "Prevention of Significant Deterioration," *Journal of the Air Pollution Control Association*, vol. 27, no. 5 (May 1977), 440–53 and Jerry Reinwand, "Study of the Evolution of Significant Deterioration," *Environment Reporter* (February 10, 1978), 1569–73.

26. See "Appeals Court Rejects EPA NSPS Stationary Source Definition," *Environment Reporter*, vol. 8, no. 40, 1500.

27. See R. Shep Melnick, *Regulation and the Courts: The Case of the Clean Air Act* (Washington: Brookings Institution, 1983), 346–47.

28. Stephen Breyer, *Regulation and Its Reform* (Cambridge: Harvard University Press, 1982), 266–69.

29. See B. Peter Pashigian, "Environmental Regulation: Whose Interests Are Being Protected?" *Economic Inquiry*, vol. 23 (October 1985), 551–84; Robert W. Crandall, *Controlling Industrial Pollution* (Washington: The Brookings Institution, 1983), 110–30; Robert Quinn and Bruce Yandle, "Expenditures on Air Pollution Control under Federal Regulation," *Review of Regional Studies*, vol. 16, no. 3 (Fall 1986), 11–16; Bruce Yandle, "Environmental Control and Regional Growth," *Growth and Change*, vol. 15, no. 3 (July 1984), 39–42; and B. Peter Pashigian, "The Effects of Environmental Regulation on Optimal Plant Size and Factor Shares," *Journal of Law and Economics*, vol. 27 (April 1984), 1–28.

30. See Michael T. Maloney and Robert E. McCormick, "A Positive Theory of Environmental Quality Regulation," *Journal of Law and Economics*, vol. 25, no. 1 (1982), 99–124.

31. See Michael T. Maloney and Gordon L. Brady, "Capital Turnover and Marketable Pollution Permits," *Journal of Law and Economics*, vol. 31, no. 1 (April 1988), 203–26.

5

Yearning for Cost Minimization

INTRODUCTION

Since the beginning of the environmental saga, if not the beginning of time, people have been aware that placing a price on something that is scarce will ration the good among competing users. A confrontation with prices enables decision makers to compare alternatives and adjust behavior to minimize costs, and spurs creative people to find substitutes for otherwise costly pursuits. Yet while those who can set prices have feelings and can discriminate, prices have no emotions and do not discriminate between people on the basis of race, nationality, political persuasion, or location.

But the impersonal nature of markets—often seen as being beneficent—is a chief problem to those hoping to predetermine outcomes. Discrimination is required, and discrimination is the stock in trade of politicians. After all, that is what interest group representation is about.

Countless books and articles on environmental economics have now been written about the use of economic incentives. Indeed, John Stewart Mill in 1862, wrote "If from any revolution in nature, the atmosphere became too scanty for the consumption, . . . air might acquire a very high marketable value."[1]

Like Mill, knowledgeable people recognize that prices—emission fees or effluent taxes—could be imposed on polluters by a benign government so that excessive use of environmental quality would be reduced and cost-effective control discovered. There is no lack of intellectual support for the isolated concept of cost effectiveness. But there is a serious lack of support for the notion when it comes to implementing the various schemes. The experience with offsets just recounted tells part of the story, but an earlier effort to use pollution taxes tells more.

In the early 1970s, the Nixon Administration made heroic efforts to tax the sulfur content of coal burned by electric utilities.[2] The notion of economic incentives was put forward on the basis of common sense logic. Electric utilities would consider the sulfur content of coal and its cost when taxed, and take actions to substitute away from burning sulfur. Sulfur oxide emissions would fall. There was also compelling evidence that the tax approach would reliably reduce sulfur oxide emissions at lower cost than by using the alternative engineering controls.

The problem encountered by the Nixon Administration was political, but not in the usual sense of the word. Congress is organized by committees. One committee was considering the tax proposal, but the Ways and Means Committee had to agree to any new tax. Spokesmen from industry knew they were opposed to taxes. They already expected to meet costly pollution control standards. A tax was seen as adding insult to injury. What they really wanted were subsidies.

The Ways and Means Committee had larger fish to fry. They had more to gain by focusing on income tax reform and the redistribution associated with it than by devoting time to an efficiency-enhancing tax on coal.

What about the environmentalists? They were generally opposed to the tax, since it seemed to say that one could buy the right to pollute, an outcome that seemed almost immoral. That community favored control by EPA, not by the IRS. EPA was sympathetic to the environmentalists and supported them; the IRS was not sympathetic to anyone.

After considerable struggle, the political limits to environmental control ended the sulfur tax proposal. Command and control conquered all parties. Following almost a decade with command control and the frustration experienced by many industrialists, environmentalists, and regulators, it is understandable that efforts to find ways to reduce control costs would again surface. EPA's offset and bubble policies emerged out of such frustration and offered the theoretical possibility of gains for all parties. But as recounted in Chapter 4, the emergence of cost-effective use of property rights, offsets, and bubbles was slow, tortuous, and in some cases almost accidental. Practically always, the inventions came from state and regional regulators, not from Washington. The Arab oil embargo forced regulators against a spiked wall. Something had to give.

In light of those events and the opportunity for congressional reform of the basic air pollution control blueprint presented by the Clean Air Act Amendments of 1977, one might think wide-open cost-effectiveness was on the way. This chapter discusses what finally developed for those who yearned for cost-effectiveness.

THE 1977 CLEAN AIR AMENDMENTS

The Clean Air Act Amendments of 1977 included a number of substantive changes that *appeared* to offer the prospects for cost minimization. But tighter new source restrictions accompanied each new window of opportunity for reducing cost. Economic incentives gained a few inches. Command and control, a few yards. The bootlegger-Baptist coalition of old sources, anti-growth environmentalists, and politicians flexed its muscles. Existing producers could increase profits by applying the new approaches, but new ones could not. They maintained important limits on the growth of newly emerging industrial regions and placated the interests of those served by the status quo.

With the 1977 Amendments, Congress allowed five more years for dirtier regions to meet the deadline for cleaning the air, a relaxation that was extended each time the next new deadline was missed. In the intervening years, Congress allowed the offset mechanism to apply to all new sources that wanted to enter a dirty region. Of course, the existing firms were the sellers in the newcomers' offset market. State politicians and bureaucrats were the brokers.

The greater than one-to-one offset remained intact, and the control technology to be used by new sources was raised to an even higher level. Before the 1977 legislation, new plants had to apply the best technology then being used to control specific pollutants. With the new law, the new plant was required to use advanced technology that had never been applied in practice. Speaking to the tightening of the regulatory screw, EPA announced:

It has been EPA's interpretation that in determining the lowest achievable emission rate (LAER), the reviewing authority may consider transfer of technology from one source type to another where such technology is applicable. Although Congress changed the definition of LAER, EPA continues to believe that technology transfer may be considered in determining LAER. Congress intended to require new sources in nonattainment areas to apply the "maximum feasible pollution control," even if this involves "technology forcing."[3]

Auctioning The Right To Pollute

The 1977 Amendments also addressed the evolution of the Prevention of Significant Deterioration (PSD) doctrine that promised protection of the cleaner air regions. Allowable pollution increments were established that assured PSD air quality would not fall to national air quality levels.

In discharging its duties under the new law, EPA turned next to the higher air quality regions and how the allowable pollution increment would be allocated. EPA's proposal for dealing with the increment encouraged the states to explore alternative allocation rules including establishing markets for pollution permits and allowing individuals to bid for them.[4] By this time, some of the environmental organizations were beginning to view market mechanisms more optimistically.

EPA's auction proposal was supported by the Environmental Defense Fund (EDF), along with some economists.[5] Speaking of the concept, EDF noted:

Traditionally, the American economic system has utilized the price system to allocate scarce resources. Land is a good example. Land is available to the individual who is willing to pay the highest price for it. The market thus allocates the land among many potential bidders. The same principle theoretically can apply to the air. The air, like the land, is a scarce commodity. There is no reason why an auction or a pricing system could not be used to distribute air emission rights, in a fashion similar to the current market which allocates land.[6]

The market-based logic of EDF's petition was faultless, but what might explain the organization's sudden appreciation for market mechanisms?

At this point it was becoming apparent that environmentalists were beginning to become discouraged with EPA's performance, still realizing that EPA was carrying out the instructions of Congress. First off, little progress was being made on the environmental front. Yet while that was recognized, exceedingly high costs were being imposed on U.S. industry. There had to be a better approach. But more to the point of the petition, EDF and others felt they could better influence a market mechanism than a political mechanism. After all, if environmentalists wanted to purchase pollution rights in an auction market and retire them, they could. As EDF noted, the potential market would be like the market for land, and everyone knew that owners often chose to hold land and not develop it. There was little chance that politicians would reserve some of the increment.

It is also important to note that EDF's petition related to the Ohio River Valley where some of the nation's largest electricity and sulfur dioxide generators were located. EDF and others predicted that politicians would allocate the Ohio River Valley's entire sulfur dioxide increment to the electrical utilities, since doing so would preserve employment in the production of the region's high sulfur-content coal production. The failure of the Nixon sulfur tax proposal returned to haunt the environmentalists.

An open market would allow for competing bidders, including EDF and other environmental organizations. Put differently, EDF was not interested in markets for the primary reason of their ability to allocate resources efficiently to the higher valued uses. Nor were they interested in cost-effectiveness for its own sake. They wanted something that would work in their interests, and that, after all, was the important force for bringing forth markets.

While EPA granted leeway for states to operate auctions for allocating pollution increments, that was not the approach utimately taken. Why should polluters want to purchase pollution rights outright when political influence might deliver the same thing at a lower price? And why would politicians and bureaucrats want to see valuable political actions auctioned to the highest bidder, when they could convert that value to campaign contributions and other gifts if given the power to allocate the valuable favors? Added to this was the political shortcoming of losing control. Unleashed markets would go their own way, leaving the politicians out of the picture. In short, the political incentives for allowing markets to emerge just weren't there. Market efficiency was one thing. Political efficiency was something else.

More on Bubbles and Offsets

The 1977 Amendments did allow EPA to go forward with bubbles and offsets, again in highly restricted ways. When EPA announced its new politically flexible bubble, the agency pointed out, "This system will reconcile improved air quality with economic growth at the least possible cost, encourage firms to develop new ways to control pollution, and enable government and industry to solve problems more flexibly.[7]" Furthermore, EPA explained that

under the alternative emission reduction concept, a source with multiple emission points (stacks, vents, ports, etc.)—each of which is subject to specific emission limitation requirements under an approved (State Plan)—may propose to meet the (plan's) total emission control . . . with a mix of controls that is different from that mandated by the existing regulation. *Sources will have the opportunity to come forward with alternative abatement strategies that would result in the same air quality impact but at less expense by placing relatively more control on emission points with a low marginal cost of control and less on emission points with a high cost.* (Emphasis added.)

Had one not known the history of air pollution control to this point, one would have thought EPA had great difficulty discovering common sense. After nine years' experience, the agency had just said polluters could minimize cost while cleaning the air.

But if this marked the arrival of common sense, its use was not to be allowed for all Americans. EPA quickly added that the new policy did not affect the rules that had to be met in the cleaner regions, nor would bubbles be allowed for new sources of pollution. Once again the pattern was clear. The entry of new competition would still be limited by the rules, and older regions would still be able to enjoy protection from loss of industry to newer regions.

How Much Advantage from Bubbles?

The competitive gain offered by bubbles was certainly not trivial and illustrates what might be gained if Congress and EPA could be dedicated to achieving maximum protection of the environment at minimum economic cost. A recent survey of studies and experience reports the ratio of costs incurred under command and control regulation to the costs generated by bubbles for the same level of control.[8] Command and control regulation is shown to be as much as twenty-two times more costly than bubbles in the best case. In the worst situation, there was a 5 percent savings.

A study of E.I. DuPont Corporation's cost of controlling gaseous hydrocarbons illustrates some additional features of bubbles.[9] Based on 1975 data for 548 sources of emissions in 52 of the firm's 102 domestic plants, the study first estimated the engineering costs of achieving an 85 percent reduction in emissions at each source, which was EPA's traditional approach to the problem. That estimate indicated that DuPont would spend $105.7 million annually to achieve 85 percent reduction.

When the same problem was solved using a bubble approach, which meant less reduction from higher–cost sources in the same plant and more reductions from lower-cost sources, the annual cost fell to $42.6 million. Going one step further, the study assumed that all the DuPont plants were located under one bubble, just for the sake of determining the cost, and that cost-minimizing adjustments could be made across all sources. In that case, the total cost fell to $14.6 million annually. Finally, the study examined the imaginary regional bubble and estimated the cost of reaching for 99 percent reduction in emissions, which was far more than EPA required. The annual cost was $92.4 million, still less than the command and control cost of achieving an 85 percent reduction.

EPA's attempts to promote bubbles, offsets, and various forms of emission trading led to an agency "bubble clearing house" and later to a separate agency office for promoting trades in what are now called "emission reduction credits." But after more than a decade's experience with some of the program, such as the offset mechanism, not much has been accomplished.[10] A review of EPA data indicates that between 5,000 and 12,000 internal trades have been made (adjustments across individual sources within the same plant), for a total cost savings of from $500 million to $12 billion. There have been 1,800 in-plant offset transactions and 200 offset transactions between different plant owners. No control cost savings are documented, but the entering plants may have gained a footing that otherwise would have been prohibited.

Through 1986 there have been only 40 air pollution bubbles approved by EPA for the entire country over the almost ten-year experience with the device. States had approved 89 additional ones. Control cost savings generated from these 129 transactions total approximately $435 million. Of course, these cost savings are surely not trivial, but the number of transactions is relatively small considering ten years of experience for the U.S. economy.

Water Bubbles

Since air bubbles created considerable excitement within EPA and among industrial firms, it seems initially curious that a similar approach did not emerge for water pollution control. In many ways, the federal blueprint for reducing and controlling water pollution paralleled that of air pollution. There were effluent guidelines that established acceptable limits on waste discharged to the nation's rivers and streams. There was a family of technology related standards that satisfied the regulator's requirements, but there were no provisions for shutting down industrial growth in regions that did not comply with the regulator's deadlines. That crucial piece was missing.

There was an additional unique characteristic of water pollution control, and it related to plumbing. Industrial plants could pipe together common pollutants and treat them. There was a natural bubble available to many industries. The gains from cost-effectiveness were not always as obvious. However, this does not mean that cost-effective control was the underlying logic of EPA action. As reported in the *1978 Economic Report of the President,* that clearly was not the case.[11] Referring to EPA's effluent guidelines for steelmaking, the report noted that the additional cost of removing one unit of the same pollutant cost $18,000 in one production process, $2,000 for another. On its face, it made little sense to pay nine times as much for the same improvement.

Source-by-source limitations were the essence of the control mechanism, and there were obvious opportunities for reducing cost. However, it was easier for imaginative plant engineers to pipe effluents to a common waste treatment plant than to perform the same task for emissions. Finally, one last important characteristic distinguished one pollution control problem from the other. It was much cheaper for the same industrial firm to control water pollution than air pollution. The latter control problem is inherently more costly.

Massive subsidies to states and municipalities for the construction of publicly owned sewage treatment works also affected the relative costs of controlling industrial waste. The 1972 Federal Water Pollution Control Act authorized grants of $9.75 billion for 1973, $6 billion for 1974, and $7.6 billion for 1975. Along with the transfers of tax monies came permission for municipalities to expand their treatment of industrial wastes.

That gave water-using industries an option for the control of wet pollution that was not available for air pollution control. Instead of installing costly control devices on plants, wet industry located near public sewers could simply pipe waste to the local sewage treatment plant.

Later federal legislation recognized that tax money was being used to subsidize the treatment of industrial waste and included requirements for industrial user charges to be made by cities. But the charges seldom reflected the full economic cost of treating waste. In any case, the demand for bubbles and other cost-effective water pollution control strategies was much weaker than for air pollution control. Still, the political economy of environmental control delivered a benefit to water-using industries along with the cost associated with tighter regulation.

Evidence of the effects of the industrial sewer subsidy was found in work we completed at Clemson in 1989.[12] We first examined state data on federal grants for the construction of municipal treatment works along with data on discharge by industry to such facilities. We found that discharge increased in association with larger transfers. We then developed a larger statistical model that estimated the effect more precisely, taking into account the years when federal law increased the charges to be paid by sewer-using industries. We found strong support for the notion that plants increased their discharge when the cost was cheaper and reduced discharge when the price went up. We finally considered the possible effect of the subsidies on the size of plants in national water-using industries and found evidence that the number of plants was increased, but their average size fell. That finding supported the idea that new plants were constructed near cities, where possible, meaning that land costs would be higher and plants smaller.

OBSTACLES TO EFFICIENCY

The emergence of offsets and bubbles marks a change in property rights, a movement from common-access use of the environment to public property managed by political appointees to a private market accommodated by government record keeping and enforcement. Each transition point in the evolution of property rights is expected to be troublesome. After all, one regime and those who gain from it is being replaced by another regime and quite possibly another group of gainers and losers.

The discussion of opposition to the new property rights approach focuses on the defenders of the status quo. Those who favor the new devices are agents for change. There are always attempts to avoid the ordeal of change. But there is another more important group that opposes the flexibility implied by marketable permits and private property rights to environmental use. Politicians and bureaucrats earn their keep by distributing valuable favors across various interest groups. Bubbles and offsets allow private agents to control who might have access to the environment and how they might use the environment. Command and control puts the power in the hands of the politicians.

There is a last consideration when thinking about why it is so difficult to introduce cost-effectiveness to environmental control. Those seeking to reduce control costs are willing to spend up to the amount saved in working their way through the political maze. The bureaucratic process is slow and costly. At some point, continuation of the effort isn't worth the additional cost. Political markets have features not found in private markets. The political broker is an absolute monopolist. And an absolute monopolist can extract all gains from the consumer. Since the political broker is a monopolist under any regulatory regime, it follows that the broker will attempt to maximize his returns, while carrying out the flexible dictates of policy. In the case of marketlike methods for controlling pollution, command and control regulation appears to be the more valuable political option.

Even though EDF supported the advent of auction markets for air pollution rights, that support turned out to be extraordinary. Typically, environmental groups have opposed marketlike mechanism in favor of command and control. As indicated previously, those special interest groups support the status quo while arguing for improvements. If Congress grants leeway to EPA, the environmental groups can struggle against the agency, bring suits, and in other ways limit the agency's actions. When combined with efforts by industrialists to delay enforcement actions and question the validity of EPA rules, litigation becomes the final product. According to a recent report of the Council on Environmental Quality, 85 percent of EPA's actions have resulted in suits brought by one group or another.[13]

Losing Sight of Goals

From all appearances, the goal of actually attaining environmental protection was lost in the struggle during the 1970s and 1980s. If it were ever foremost in their minds, the contentious parties seemed to lose sight of the official purpose of the environmental saga—progress in cleaning the environment. Finding the least cost path toward that goal was lost in the struggle as well, which is understandable when the goal of cleaning the environment becomes less important than providing valuable political support to one group or another.

Environmental quality is convenient clothing that hides other important objectives. It is understandable that regulations for reducing sulfur dioxide from the boilers of electricity generators pay attention to employment effects on coal miners in the east, specify that reductions must be made, yet in final form pay no attention to control costs.[14] In a similar way, it seems more reasonable that new source standards would be set very high, while allowing existing polluters to operate older plants that continue to pollute the environment. As a result, only marginal improvements are achieved in air quality, if any gains are made at all. Special interests get served, but the general interest in environmental quality is offered unicorns.

SUMMARY

An examination of efforts to generate cost-effective pollution control shows no lack of interest and effort on the part of major players in the environmental saga. Efforts were made from the very beginning. But each struggle has been frustrated by bootlegger-Baptist coalitions. Still, some progress has been made, though the progress usually seems larger when described in the work of environmental economists.

The yearning for cost effectiveness continues in some quarters, and economic stress from outside the environmental arena occasionally forces the issue to resurface. All in all, the saga to this day continues to be driven by command and control where political considerations override economic efficiency.

NOTES

1. John Stewart Mill, *Principles of Political Economy* (London: Lambe Publishing, 1862 edition).

2. See Paul B. Downing, *Environmental Economics and Policy* (Boston: Little, Brown and Company, 1984); and William A. Irwin and Richard A. Liroff, *Economic Disincentives for Pollution Control: Legal, Political and Administrative Dimensions*, EPA-600/5–74–026 (Washington: U.S. Environmental Protection Agency, 1974.)

3. See U.S. EPA, "Emission Offset Interpretative Ruling," *Federal Register*, vol. 44, no. 11 (January 16, 1979), 3280.

4. See U.S. EPA, "Prevention of Significant Deterioration," *Federal Register*, vol. 43, no. 118 (June 19, 1978), 26381.

5. For a discussion of EDF's petition and other related points, see Bruce Yandle, "Buying and Selling for Cleaner Air?" *Business*, vol. 29, no. 2 (March/April 1979), 33–36.

6. Environmental Defense Fund, "Petition for the Initiation of Rulemaking Proceedings to Insure Maintenance of the National Ambient Air Quality Standards and the Prevention of Significant Deterioration Increments in the Ohio River Valley," presented before the U.S. Environmental Protection Agency (Washington, D.C.: Environmental Defense Fund, July 17, 1978).

7. See U.S. EPA, "Air Pollution Control: Recommendations for Alternative Emission Reduction Options within State Implementation Plans," *Federal Register*, vol. 44, no. 13 (January 18, 1979); Timothy B. Clark, "New Approaches to Regulatory Reform—Letting the Market Do the Job," *National Journal* (August 11, 1979), 1316–1322; Peter Nulty, "A Brave Experiment in Pollution Control," *Fortune* (February 12, 1979), 120–23; and "The 'Bubble Concept': Industry Chance to Innovate Best-Buy Air Pollution Control," *Congressional*

Action, vol. 23, no. 3 (Washington: Chamber of Commerce of the U.S., September 14, 1979), 5.

8. See Tom Tietenberg, *Environmental and Natural Resource Economics*, Sec. Ed. (Glenview, Ill: Scott, Foresman and Company, 1988), 346–48. Also, by the same author, *Emissions Trading: An Exercise in Reforming Pollution Policy* (Washington: Resources for the Future, 1985).

9. See T.A. Kittleman and R.B. Akell, "The Cost of Controlling Organic Hydrocarbons," *Chemical Engineering Progress* (April 1978), 87–91; and M.T. Maloney and Bruce Yandle, "Estimation of the Cost of Air Pollution Control Regulation," *Journal of Environmental Economics and Management*, vol. 11 (1984), 244–63.

10. For a recent survey of actual EPA experience, see Robert W. Hahn, "Economic Prescriptions for Environmental Problems: Not Exactly What the Doctor Ordered," *Journal of Economic Perspectives*, forthcoming.

11. *Economic Report of the President, 1978* (Washington: Government Printing Office, January 1978), 212.

12. The work referred to here is Anand Bhansali, Charles Diamond, and Bruce Yandle, "Sewers as Subsidies," Department of Economics (Clemson University, January 1989).

13. See Council on Environmental Quality, *Environmental Quality, 1985* (Washington: Council on Environmental Quality, 1988), 2–3.

14. See Bruce Ackerman and G. Hassler, *Clean Coal/Dirty Air* (New Haven: Yale University Press, 1981), a detailed recounting of the struggle by EPA to develop emission control guidelines for new coal-fired generators, a struggle that ended with the adoption of the most costly control alternative considered and the possibility for little if any reduction in SO^2 emissions.

6

The Move to Manage
Hazardous and Toxic Wastes

INTRODUCTION

The review of regulatory activity spawned by the 1970 Clean
Air Act and the 1972 Federal Water Pollution Control Act and
their later amendments shows that the actions were designed
to reduce pollution discharged by industries and cities, as well
as from automobiles. Concern about pollution was obviously
based on harm that might be imposed on people, potential
hazards that could make life riskier. But there was considerable and sometimes greater concern registered about harm
that might be done directly to the natural environment, the
ecological system. Indeed, analysts who attempted to place
the regulatory actions in a risk analysis framework were
often rebuffed, since risk reduction involves comparisons of
alternatives, levels of control, and trade-offs. Such technical
treatment of an emotional topic was destined to meet harsh
opposition.

Perhaps the emerging focus on toxic materials and risk reduction came when it was recognized that even with all its
wealth, America did not have the resources to reduce pollution to zero, that like it or not, priorities would have to be
ordered. Clearly, one seeking to maximize the benefits of the
environmental saga would list exposure to toxic wastes above
exposure to inert materials that reduced the aesthetic quality

of life. That is precisely what happened as amendments were added later to the basic pollution control statutes.

The emphasis on the control of toxic wastes in discharge that went into publicly owned treatment works, the oceans, and rivers was just another part of command and control regulation. All along, however, one form of pollution, be it air or water, was being transformed into other forms of waste that had to be disposed of. Encouraging wet process industries to inject wastes underground increased the possibility of damaging aquifers that are major sources of drinking water. Along with these tendencies came intense studies of potential hazards that related to the movement of chemicals from one production point to another and the ultimate disposal of wastes.

Common law safeguards provided protection to owners of property damaged by those who dumped harmful waste. But there was no common law protection for the public domain—the rights of way of highways, public lands, beaches, and abandoned disposal sites that lacked management with ownerlike concern. Rules addressing the problem of how to manage the distribution of risky materials and what to do about old sites where toxic materials might have been dumped were substantially different from those that addressed the processing of new products.

LOVE CANAL AND SUPERFUND

Just the mention of hazardous wastes and chemical dumps automatically conjures up images of Love Canal, Hooker Chemical Company, and hardworking middle class Americans who found toxic wastes oozing up in their basements.[1] To the average person, the issue is clear-cut. Hooker Chemical is the culprit. The local residents are the victims. Government is the rescuer.

The location: Niagara Falls, New York. The time of extensive public notice: August 1978, when President Carter declared the Love Canal community the site of a national emergency. The effect: The necessary momentum to pass the

Comprehensive Environmental Response, Compensation, and Liability Act of 1980, which established Superfund.

This is the popular view of the Love Canal episode, and part of it holds up under close scrutiny. Sadly, however, a major part of the story does not, and the misconceptions associated with the errors have been costly.

For example, many people believe Hooker Chemical Company owned and operated the Love Canal dump right up to the time of the calamity that affected many unsuspecting homeowners. That is not the case. The canal and adjoining land had been sold by Hooker in 1953, some twenty-five years before the calamity, to the Niagara Falls School Board following threats by the board to take the land through eminent domain proceedings. Hooker knew exactly what was stored in the sealed canal, had taken precautions to protect the site that would satisfy even today's high standards, gave public warnings of the hazards involved, and wrote extensive covenants and caveats in the deed of sale that precluded any future land use that would threaten human health. All of this is in the public record.

What happened? The School Board developed the land for a grammar school and then sold remaining parcels to real estate developers, somehow doing so without the stringent deed restrictions. The rest of the story follows the popular line. When sewer lines were laid to serve the new residential area, the sealed canal was ruptured. Heavy rains flushed toxic wastes into the soil. Percolation did the rest. Eventually, toxic sludge was showing up on the property and in the lower levels of homes in the area.

Not one person was harmed severely by exposure to the waste. No adverse health effects have been found, even after extensive efforts to make a determination by a panel of scientists assembled by Governor Hugh Carey, the New York State Department of Health, and the Centers for Disease Control.[2] But all this is beside the point. The waste was in people's homes. Property losses were significant. There was immense emotional distress. The waste had been produced and stored by Hooker. They were sued by the

Department of Justice on behalf of EPA and by the affected property owners. Hooker settled the suit for $20 million. The local government and School Board were let off the hook. Today, Hooker Chemical is still viewed as the villain in the piece.

Love Canal is interesting in its own right, but of greater importance because of the episode's impact on popular opinion and on Congress. Legislation for regulating hazardous waste sites had been debated, but something like Love Canal was needed to get the politicians rolling. Given the nature of the problem, what could be more logical than establishing an insurance fund with risk premiums based on hazardous waste produced, stored, and abandoned, wastes that could later damage property and human health? The funds would be used only in those cases where the producer of the waste was no longer on the scene, for the so-called orphan sites, where the responsible party was either bankrupt or no longer in existence.

A host of forgotten nasty sites that posed significant hazards to innocent people could be cleared away using payments from the insurance proceeds. Where possible, liability would be assigned to the original site operator, those who carted the waste there, and ultimately on the producer of the waste, when any one or all of these could be found. And since waste is fungible and the identity of the party responsible for it not easily determined, all of the potential culprits would be jointly and severally liable. The insurance idea would handle sins of the past.

Regulatory safeguards for current operators of landfills and waste sites had been included in the 1974 Resource Conservation and Recovery Act, which imposed cradle to grave rules on generators, carriers, and operators of disposal sites.[3] These rules were strengthened further by the 1984 Hazardous and Solid Waste Amendments, which banned outright the land disposal and underground injection of certain specified chemicals. The 1984 Amendments required EPA to consider banning the land disposal of a list of chemical wastes and required an automatic ban if EPA did not complete its review in a timely fashion.

CERCLA AND SUPERFUND

To deal with sins of the past, Congress passed the Comprehensive Environmental Response, Compensation, and Liability Act (CERCLA) on December 11, 1980 and with it established Superfund. The statute set up a Hazardous Response Fund to be used to pay the cleanup costs.[4] The fund was set at $1.6 billion and was to receive 87.5 percent of its revenues from taxes on petroleum and forty-two listed chemical feedstocks. The balance was provided from general tax revenues.[5]

To implement Superfund, the law required EPA to establish a National Priorities List of at least 400 sites and in doing so to call on the states to submit candidate sites. EPA was required to include each state's top priority in its top 400, without weighing the relative risk imposed by the state sites. In other words, all of the sites in one state might be more hazardous than any of the sites in another state, yet a less hazardous site from one state would displace a more hazardous site from another state.

CERCLA was a technocrat's dream, but an insurance fund operator's and economist's nightmare. Fault crept into and overwhelmed a process that should have been a public works project. Wastes from the past need to be cleaned up, if that is what citizen-taxpayers want. Laws affecting current and future behavior, like RCRA, should then be enforced strictly to avoid the same kinds of problems, again if that is what citizen-taxpayers want. There is no overall economic reason to find responsible parties whose past legal behavior now poses a problem. But there was a narrow economic reason for doing so, just as there was for using regulation to clean up the nation's air and waterways.

It is never in a politician's interest to raise taxes, as evidenced by the federal deficit. When caught in the jaws of a fiscal vise, Congress has to find innovative ways to fund new constituent benefits. The combination of a tax on new production of chemical products, based on feed stocks, and liability for cleaning up old wastes, combined with an infusion of some taxpayer money gave a double whammy to liable firms and a bonanza to any local communities that got their dumps and landfills on the Superfund list.

THE INSURANCE PROBLEM

Though often viewed as an insurance-based solution to the problem of orphan sites, Superfund is clearly not that. Insurance deals with identifiable risks, uncertain events that accidentally befall the insured party in the normal course of doing business. With experience, the insurer can estimate the probability of the event's occurring, set a premium, and fund losses for a large group of insured parties. The policy pays when an accident covered by the policy occurs. Those who are extra careful receive discounts, ideally never having to pay for the faulty behavior of others.

Competition among private insurance carriers promotes cost-effective controls, leads to the systematic collection of data on risks, and imposes risk-reducing management practices on insured parties. In contrast, there is obviously no direct competition on Superfund insurance, which is mandated by federal law. EPA, the operator of the fund, is basically a monopolist and therefore has no economic incentive to minimize costs.

CERCLA destroyed the insurance principle on several counts. First and foremost, the cleanup event is not a random occurrence. It is a political event and is not related to an accident. There's no way to estimate the likelihood of occurrence. If anything, the premiums paid to Superfund are simply payments advanced to cover a totally unknown future cost. Going on, the risk premiums paid by chemical producers are constant across firms, no matter what the Superfund experience. There's no differential cost incentive to promote more cautious behavior. And since the Superfund tax is not experience based, there's no reason to gather data on the relative riskiness of the products subject to the tax. A major stimulus is missing for improving risk assessment, an artistic science at best.

The joint and several liability feature of CERCLA also undermines the insurance concept, yet on the surface seems to increase EPA's chances of recovering cleanup costs from private parties. As it stands, one firm out of 100 can be found financially liable for the entire cost of cleaning a site, even if the one firm contributed the smallest part of the waste. There's a tendency to go for the deep pockets.

Firms with the deepest pockets, such as major chemical companies, have far more at stake than just the funds set aside for legal contingencies. They have their international reputations at stake. Brand name capital is one of their major assets. Unlike operators of a local landfill, the major chemical companies must consider the expected losses of shareholder wealth that accompanies bad publicity and open-ended liability. They face more than the costs of an isolated legal suit and associated penalties. Joint and several liability binds the larger firms to smaller ones, increasing the potential amount recovered by EPA yet simultaneously raising the stakes in litigation. It is not clear that the after-legal-costs proceeds are increased.

Finally, a standard piece of liability contract language has been violated by the courts. Individuals have been allowed to recover from their liability insurance for damages to their own property. That introduces a severe moral hazard problem. Under these circumstances, few insurance firms are eager to write contracts designed to give future indemnification for chemical companies and operators of landfills and waste-processing facilities. There are too many unknowns.

How Bad Is the Insurance Problem?

We have to step away from Superfund and related hazardous waste legislation to gain an appreciation of the problems posed by environmental regulation to commercial insurance companies. In the 1970s, when the environmental movement was fundamentally an antibusiness movement, New York legislators got the idea that having liability insurance pay claims for pollution spills just made it easier for firms to continue their bad habits.[6] Other New York officials pointed out to no avail that liability insurance was no escape for bad actors. Their point was a simple one: Just like unsafe drivers, bad polluters would pay higher premiums for liability insurance. In the long run, those costs like all others would be borne by the polluter's customers, and firms with a bad record on pollution-generated costs would suffer in the marketplace. The desired market pressures would be delivered by the insurance vehicle, not eliminated by it.[7] Nonetheless, in 1971 Governor Nelson A. Rockefeller signed a statute making it unlawful for insurance companies to offer liability coverage for pollution-induced property damages. At the time, he indicated the action would preclude insurance companies from "undermining public policy."[8]

Since New York is a major insurance state, it is little wonder that the insurance industry vacated the pollution insurance market. Denial of the market experience carried a longer run cost. With no insurance product, there was no reason to process risk information regarding the pollution hazard. All that was reversed by RCRA in 1976 and Love Canal and Superfund later. In 1982, New York repealed its law, and the federal teeth of RCRA required operators of landfills, landfill treatment facilities, and surface impoundments—like Love Canal—to carry liability insurance. But for all practical purposes insurers have ceased to offer environmental coverage.

The insurers suffered through experiences with Superfund litigation where judges disregarded insurance contract language that limited coverage to sudden and accidental spills and forced insurers to pay for damages caused by slow seepages and poorly managed facilities.[9]

Disregard of mutually agreed on contract language was just too much. Few firms could rationally price open-ended liability insurance. By 1987 just one insurance company was actively marketing pollution liability insurance in the United States.[10] In the same year, EPA estimated there were 100,000 firms generating hazardous wastes, and all are required to meet financial responsibility guidelines that require either insurance or a showing of financial strength for meeting potential pollution liabilities.

Although the effects of the insurance demise on the chemical and waste handling industries have not been documented, it is fairly obvious that smaller firms are at a competitive disadvantage when a lack of insurance availability and RCRA requirements force them to self-insure for a minimum of $6 million annually in losses. Smaller firms can pool their risks with other firms, but the effect on the marginal firm will be felt. Hazardous waste regulation, like air and water pollution regulation before it, placed a heavier relative burden on smaller firms.

Referring to the failed attempt to introduce pollution exclusions in insurance contracts and the expansive interpretations of liability made by courts, Bradford Rich examined the explosion of litigation that later emerged.[11] Rich illustrated the problem by referring to a New Jersey landfill case where a municipality was alleged to have erred in selecting and operating the site.[12] As a result, pollution seeped into an underground aquifer and polluted ninety-seven privately owned wells. The city sued its insurer for recovery of costs, but the insurance contract had the standard language. It provided coverage for accidental spills only. In spite of that, the court ruled in favor of the municipality, stating that the exclusion was clear, but that the damage was not expected, which meant it was accidental.

The same case illustrates how insurance firms can face a multiplier effect when their contract language is disregarded. The standard policy limits the total damages to be paid for each occurrence covered by the policy. The court first required the insurance firm to pay for an event it had excluded in the contract and then interpreted the policy's occurrence limitation to mean per claim, not per occurrence. In other words, the numerous parties can claim damage from one occurrence, and the limits will be applied to each party, not to the total of all claims.

The ninety-seven well owners were initially awarded a total of $15.9 million for their losses, with $2.1 million being the payment for emotional distress that accompanied the knowledge that their wells were contaminated. A total of $5.4 million was paid for the deterioration of quality of life for the twenty months when the plaintiffs were deprived of running water.

An award of $8.2 million was made to cover medical surveillance activities for those thought to be harmed. On appeal, the higher court upheld the interpretation of the contract but reduced the total damages to $5.4 million, noting there was no evidence of any harmful health effects.

When courts regularly take such actions, it is only natural that insurance firms and those they represent will spend large sums of money on litigation. Simple benefit-cost analysis says they will spend some part of the expected court-imposed costs on litigation. The American Insurance Association retained a consulting firm to determine just how much those litigation costs would be for Superfund activities alone.[13] The consultants assumed that 1,800 sites will eventually be placed on the Superfund list, which is a conservative number according to EPA, and the average cleanup cost will run $8.1 million, giving a total of $14.9 billion. Drawing on recent litigation costs per site, the consultants found that total litigation expenditures will run at least $8 billion, or 55 percent of the direct cost of cleaning the sites. Of the $8 billion, 79 percent will be paid by private parties. Elimination of litigation would release enough resources to clean more than 400 additional sites.

How can litigation costs be pushed to zero? And who would favor such an outcome? Simplifying CERCLA by eliminating joint and several liability would go a long way, since that would lower the stakes for each potentially liable party. Legislation that caps the total to be paid and that tightens the statute of limitations on suits to be brought could also contribute to a reduction of courtroom battles. But the major players do not find it in their interest to bring these changes.

The insurance industry has generally abandoned the market. Large firms can self-insure, which has the effect of limiting competition from the more vulnerable small firms. The law firms that represent the potentially liable parties make their livings fighting in court. The longer the battle, the higher the fees. Of course, there are competitive safeguards in just how far law firms can go in all this. Only the mass of unorganized consumers might gain from changes to reduce litigation, and they represent a weaker coalition than the environmental organizations that are pushing for even stronger Superfund language. The day for cost-effective change has not arrived.

User Fees and Superfund

In a way, it is paradoxical that Superfund would fail on cost-effectiveness grounds.[14] At first blush, the tax on feedstocks and petroleum should generate a search for less hazardous substitutes on the part of chemical producers. But as mentioned earlier, major elements of an ideal pollution tax are missing. The tax gives no consideration to the chemical producer's environmental record, has no linkage to the costs and benefits of pollution control, and its proceeds are used in ways that induce strategic behavior on the part of public citizens who simply want a cleaner world. The lack of linkages to benefits and costs and the failure to consider the relative riskiness of producer behavior are enough to bankrupt the efficiency aspects of the Superfund tax. But relative to strategic behavior, those two flaws are minor imperfections.

The incentives that derive from the tax, or what might be termed the Superfund user fee, cause citizens who want more action to rally their efforts. Demanders of cleanup action are not charged directly when seeking to gain recognition. At the margin, political action is a free good to them. Since firms are paying, but citizen groups are not, there is a serious imbalance in the political market for Superfund action. If both sides faced a similar price, the forces would balance more predictably.

But then the accumulation in the Superfund itself sets off another set of incentives. Since those who receive benefits from remedial action are not linked to the cost of that action, they obviously want a larger Superfund. Discussions about raising the tax on producers are logically and cheerfully supported by all who have a waste site in reasonable proximity to their homes. Indeed, one and all would be expected to support cleanliness, which is after all next to godliness.

Given these incentives, the Superfund temptation is more than Congress can suppress. Environmentalists and ordinary citizens can be rallied when figures of authority talk about toxic chemicals and carcinogens that might be contaminating the local water supply. That pressure generates demand for more actions, higher taxes, and other political support for dealing with what appears to be an environmental catastrophe.

These incentive-borne actions seemed to come to fruition when Congress evaluated EPA's Superfund record. Deeply disappointed with progress under the original Superfund legislation, Congress was made aware of the insurance demise and related issues when Superfund reauthorization was debated in 1985–86, but none of the insurance crippling features were changed. Instead, Congress took the regulatory burden on itself, tightened timetables, increased appropriations and Superfund taxes, and opened the door wider for the inclusion of additional sites.[15] Under the Superfund Amendments and Reauthorization Act of 1986 (SARA), EPA must begin remedial work at a rate of not less than 175 sites annually through 1989. The agency is mandated to speed up its internal review of candidate sites, without considering the relative risks across sites. But more to the point of this discussion of citizen action and incentives, SARA assures a long life to Superfund by authorizing private parties to petition EPA to perform risk assessments on any site, whether or not the site has been placed on the national priority listing. Further controversy is assured by SARA requirements that Superfund site communities be given grants for the purpose of contesting EPA's selected cleanup remedies.

WILL COST EFFECTIVENESS COME INTO VOGUE?

Even the most optimistic policy analyst would find it difficult to predict when, if ever, cost considerations will enter Superfund and related activities. Experience with the older environmental programs, like air pollution control, suggests that efficiency concerns take hold when there is a collision between the law and the economic fortunes of an important region, major state, or industry. But when the economy is moving at a very healthy pace, everything seems possible—even an expanded Superfund. Just what are the dimensions of the program? Is it conceivable that Superfund will ever end, that all the sites will eventually be cleaned and forgotten? Even before SARA expanded the range of Superfund activities, the outlook was bleak.

As a statement from a 1985 congressional staff report on the status of Superfund programs summarized the problem, "It is clear from the accumulating data on waste sites that EPA will never have adequate monies and manpower to address the problem [of all hazardous waste sites] itself."[16]

In March 1988, the *Environment Reporter* summarized a House Appropriations Committee staff report on Superfund and noted that the $8.5 billion fund will fall short of the amount needed to clean the 951 sites currently targeted by EPA.[17] So far, EPA has found it far more appealing to draw on Superfund instead of going after the potentially liable parties for cost recovery. Litigation costs are high, and the process drones on for years. Meanwhile, EPA avoids political pressure by moving ahead under its own steam. Even at its own pace, the cleanup procedure takes years. Just the studies associated with preparing to clean a site take five years on average.

In 1988 the average cleanup cost of a Superfund site was running between $21 and $30 million. At that rate, from $16 to $24 billion is needed to fund the sites *currently* targeted for action. But those 951 sites are only the beginning. EPA has currently more than 27,000 candidate sites for the Superfund program, and more are added on a regular basis. It is obvious that most of the 27,000 will not make the grade, but some will. If the Superfund cannot handle 951 sites, how can more be added? Maybe the proverbial handwriting is on the wall. Maybe economic reality will overwhelm political rhetoric.

As currently constituted, Superfund and CERCLA make an attractive politician's pork barrel. Demand for EPA's services far exceeds supply. Politicians can put on shining armor and make a name for themselves with the homefolks by bringing home the bacon. But unlike traditional pork barrel projects (like dams, canals, bridges, and roads), whether justified or not, Superfund sites stir a deep emotion among people who live near them. It is exceedingly difficult politically to turn off the Superfund faucet after convincing people that they are at risk.

Sanity and Proposition 65

Past experience with federal environmental regulation teaches us that meaningful progress will not likely be found when we assess the record of accomplishments. An examination of the institutions, the rules, regulations, and political incentives helps us to understand why. We have earlier reviewed the tortuous path followed under the programs designed to deal with air and water pollution, the conventional pollutants. And we have traced the implementation of laws that address risks associated with hazardous waste. Cost effective control finally forced itself into air and water pollution control when the impossibility of meeting mandated standards was obvious. Should we expect the same thing for the control of hazardous chemicals?

As strange as it may seem, California's Proposition 65 is an important indicator that rationality may soon arrive. When that state's Safe Drinking Water and Toxic Enforcement Act of 1986 became effective on March 1, 1988, California citizens were greeted with an endless array of warnings.[18] Whether selecting canned goods in the grocery store, filling the family sedan with gasoline, or dropping off clothes at the corner dry cleaners, the warnings are the same: The items sold or services provided contain chemicals shown to be hazardous to human health. Everything from wine, beer, table salt, mushrooms, herbal tea, peanut butter, and even drinking water from typical waterworks fail to make the grade. Each item contains chemicals, in some cases natural ones, that are carcinogens.

California has drawn some bright lines, setting a minimum risk standard that cannot be exceeded without providing the mandatory warnings. As a consequence, people are learning that life has been risky all along, yet somehow people have done more than survive and prosper. Life expectancies have increased. Most likely, however, the overflow of warnings will ultimately provide little information at all. It will be difficult to make comparative evaluations, because practically everything will carry the same warnings.

But the abundance of warnings may bring a new recognition that risks cannot be totally avoided. Common sense and good management are required. Priorities will have to be set on some rational basis, most likely and logically at the community level. That makes cost effectiveness all the more appealing.

Proposition 65 is based on the notion that drinking water will have to be protected from contaminated aquifers, which is the logic of CERCLA and RCRA. But the thrust of the law suggests this can be done exclusively by tightening the controls on the production and disposal of man-made chemicals. Bruce N. Ames, Professor and Chairman of the Department of Biochemistry at Berkeley and the acknowledged expert on the subject, testified before the California Senate on the proposed legislation and argued that the Proposition 65 approach is totally misdirected. He even went so far as to say that the levels of carcinogens and pesticide residues found in California water are an irrelevant cause of human cancer.[19]

Ames pointed out that 99.99 percent of the carcinogens ingested by Californians are from natural and traditional sources, chemicals that include insecticides produced naturally by plants and common sources like cigarettes, alcohol, and chemicals formed in cooking food.[20] As to contaminated drinking water, Ames indicated that the level of carcinogens in contaminated wells in Silicon Valley only rarely exceeded that of chlorinated city tap water. Oddly enough, hysteria-induced switching from well to city drinking water could increase, not decrease, health risks.

The right to know requirements under Superfund amendments parallel Proposition 65 to some extent. When local citizens become bombarded with information about chemicals that are produced, stored, and shipped from all processing plants in their communities, they too will suffer from information overload. A first reaction will likely combine fear and outrage. But most people will soon realize that nothing is really new. In most cases, the risks will have been there for years. Only the information is new.

A final indicator of the possibilities that rationality might take hold and finally give direction to the massive expenditure of resources underway was seen recently in an EPA effort to order its own priorities.[21] Trying to find its own baseline, the EPA established a team of seventy-five agency professionals and gave them a mandate to review all major EPA programs as they relate to human health, to see just how well the agency was matching resources to health risk problems.

The results of that study revealed that large expenditures by EPA do not square at all with large risks to human health. Indeed, some of the agency's major programs are associated with some of the smallest risks, whereas some major health risks receive small commitments of resources. The report went on to explain why this odd outcome is logical after all. EPA responds to political pressure, which is partly affected by public perceptions of risks. In other words, EPA does what Congress directs it to do, and Congress has a complex agenda. But putting all this forward in a methodical fashion suggests that cost effectiveness is at least being considered by the lead environmental control agency.

BUREAUCRATS AND POLITICAL ECONOMY

The Superfund shortfall results from a combination of bureaucratic and pork barrel motivations. According to congressional reports, EPA bureaucrats prefer to keep Superfund activities under their thumbs, instead of going after private parties who might be found responsible for the problem and therefore liable for the cost of cleanup. The predictable bureaucratic tendency, which feeds the professional ambitions of dedicated staff and inevitably generates calls for larger budgets, is reinforced by the high cost of litigation and the long delays associated with that process. This centralizing effect feeds the political machinery in Congress. EPA is the whipping boy, never meeting the impossible deadlines nor doing enough to satisfy the politicians. Industry is the villain, and the flaming emotions of innocent people are fanned by the rhetoric that ensues. Heated hearings, more proposed laws, larger budgets, and limited progress is the result. Political demand continues to outstrip political supply.

The same congressional staff report that pessimistically announced that EPA could never accomplish the goals set for it provided more optimistic information on what one state was doing with its Superfund program.[22] According to the report, Minnesota passed a state superfund law in 1983, originally appropriating $5 million for funding it, which was later supplemented with $9.4 million. Sources of funds for the $9.4 million include $3.9 million in tax monies, $3.5 million in reimbursements and penalties, and $2 million in interest earned on the fund itself. The state program lists 130 sites to be cleaned, including 36 on EPA's Superfund list.

Started in 1983, the Minnesota program now lists 20 of its 130 sites as having a final cleanup in place, some 15 percent. At the national level, EPA has 13 of its 951 sites at that point, slightly more than one percent. Minnesota has 70 staff workyears committed to its program. EPA has 2,000. While the comparison cannot be pushed too far, it is interesting that Minnesota pushes responsible parties to take on the studies and the cleanup, while EPA does the reverse. Of course, the Minnesota superfund operators neither deal with Congress nor do they have the ability to print money. Perhaps, the reality spawned by a budget constraint has as much to do with Minnesota's relative success as anything else.

Questioning the Premise of Superfund

Even if all the faults of Superfund mentioned here could somehow be corrected, at least partially, it is highly doubtful that the program should be continued. It's a matter of priorities. Although some of the risks addressed by Superfund are real, there are even greater health risks that could be reduced by spending far less. Unfortunately, environmental protection in the United States occurs on a piecemeal basis. In the process, air pollution is considered at one time, water degradation at another, and then hazardous waste and toxic chemicals have their day. Each legislative battle is a major undertaking. Battle lines get drawn to separate the advocates of particular programs from the opposition. Protecting human health and extending life expectancies from all publicly funded programs taken together receives no consideration.

Paul Portney, former senior economist with the Council on Environmental Quality, recently stated the argument for an overall view in persuasive terms.[23] Hitting the problem head-on, he first recommended that EPA apply the cost-effective bubble concept to risks instead of to emissions of waste. To do that, the environmental regulators would have to scan an array of threats to human health, consider the resource costs for dealing with each, and then allocate resources to those activities that reduce risks the most. Atmospheric air pollution might be the gravest threat in some locations, radon emissions in others, hazardous dumps at a third. Priorities would differ geographically, depending on the toxicity of the pollutant and human exposure. Instead of being labeled the maximum allowable pollution to be discharged under the social bubble, the label would read human risk. Costly attention now devoted to piecemeal legislative and courtroom battles would be focused on human health, the presumed purpose of the environmental control enterprise.

Portney then addresses the Superfund program and basically writes it off as a waste of resources, but not a complete waste. This is his point: Superfund is a pork barrel that does not focus on reducing risk to human beings. Although some risks are reduced, this is accomplished at an extremely high cost. There are more fertile fields for risk reduction to be worked long before getting to Superfund.

EXAMINING THE DATA

It is relatively easy to review the short history of the Superfund program, appeal to theories of bureaucratic behavior, and then conclude that Superfund is just another political pork barrel. The task of assessing data and finding support for the proposition is far more difficult. Two pieces of empirical research have examined EPA's identification of Superfund sites, the resulting expenditures on those sites, and the contributions made for firms to the Superfund itself. The evidence that political power tilts the process is unambiguously strong.

The first study reviewed the operation of EPA's Hazard Ranking System, which is used by the agency to determine Superfund program status for candidate sites.[24] Data on EPA decisions to commit remediation funds to sites for 1981–83 were assembled that reflected the agency's own determination of the riskiness of various sites. The agency's criteria for selection involved rankings of hazards associated with ground water, surface water, air quality, and a composite of those three factors.

The research estimated the statistical relationship between those factors and EPA's final selection of sites. Other factors included in the statistical work had to do with state participation in cleanup programs, the commitment of state and federal resources to sites, and levels of enforcement activities across states.

The results of the study are interesting for several reasons. First, there is strong evidence that EPA's selection criteria work for some dimensions of the selection process. The agency is more likely to commit dollars where surface water and air pollution problems are associated with a hazardous waste site. But the second feature of the results cuts the other way. Where pollution of groundwater is a threat, which is the underlying concern that gave rise to Superfund, the agency is less likely to commit funds. In other words, serious groundwater pollution problems receive fewer dollars in the decision-making process. Something else is driving the system.

The second study examines the contribution of tax monies to Superfund by the chemical industry.[25] Plants that use more hazardous chemicals and petroleum pay more taxes, since it is believed that those firms pose greater threats to environmental quality. It is assumed that funds paid on a geographic basis will be spent in the same region, since that is where the disposal of associated wastes occurs.

An examination of 1985 tax data and EPA expenditures on sites for the fifty states reveals the reverse of what might be expected. Where tax payments are highest, EPA expenditures are lowest. Simply put, the Superfund program redistributes dollars from states where production occurs to states that have little chemical production. The results suggest that the chemical industry takes care of its disposal problems in the regions where plants are located. But other problems, not related to chemical production—such as the cleaning of old municipal waste sites in far away states—are addressed with revenues paid by the chemical producers.

Evidence that Superfund is a pork barrel program does not deny the fact that EPA is working to clear away old waste and clean up the environment. However, the statistical findings coupled with data from many other reports suggest that CERCLA and Superfund are high cost approaches for dealing with low priority problems.

NOTES

1. This discussion draws on Peter Huber, "Environmental Hazards and Liability Law," Robert E. Litan and Clifford Winston, eds., *Liability Perspectives and Policy* (Washington: The Brookings Institution, 1988), 128–54; Eric Zuesse, "Love Canal: The Truth Seeps Out," *Reason* (February 1981), 17–33; and Raymond A. Rea, "Hazardous Waste Pollution: The Need for a Different Statutory Approach," *Environmental Law*, vol. 12 (1982), 443–67.

2. See Fred L. Smith, "Superfund: A Hazardous Waste of Taxpayer Money," *Human Events* (August 2, 1986), 662–71.

3. For discussion, see *Environmental Law Handbook*, 8th ed. (Rockville, Maryland: Government Institute, Inc., 1985), 61.

4. See "Superfund: A Game of Chance," *Natural Resources and Environment*, vol. 1, no. 3 (Fall 1985), a symposium issue.

5. See *Environmental Law Handbook*, 8th ed. (Rockville, Maryland: Government Institute, Inc., 1985), 134.

6. See Eugene R. Anderson and Avraham C. Moskowitz, "How Much Does the CGL Pollution Exclusion Really Exclude?" *Risk Management* (August 1984), 29–34.

7. The point is developed extensively in Martin T. Katzman, *Chemical Catastrophes: Regulating Environmental Risk Through Pollution Insurance* (Homewood, Ill.: Richard D. Irwin, Inc., 1985).

8. Anderson and Moskowitz, "How Much Does the CGL Pollution Exclusion Really Exclude?" 30.

9. See Peter Huber, "The Environmental Liability Dilemma," *CPCU Journal* (December 1987), 206–16.

10. U.S. General Accounting Office, "Hazardous Waste: Issues Surrounding Insurance Availability," GAP/RCED-88–2 (Washington: U.S. General Accounting Office, October 1987).

11. See Bradford W. Rich, "Environmental Litigation and the Insurance Dilemma," *Risk Management* (December 1985), 34–41.

12. Ibid., 34.

13. Ibid., 41.

14. The discussion here is based on Bruce Yandle, "A Public Choice Interpretation of Environmental User Charges and Superfund," *Cato Journal* (forthcoming).

15. See James J. Florio, "Congress as Reluctant Regulators: Hazardous Waste Policy in the 1980s," *Yale Journal on Regulation*, vol. 3, no. 2 (Spring 1986), 351–82.

16. Survey and Investigations Staff, "A Report to the Committee on Appropriations, U.S. House of Representatives, on the Status of the Environmental Protection Agency's Superfund Program" (March 1988), 9.

17. "Current Developments," *Environment Reporter* (March 25, 1988), 25.

18. For a recent general discussion, see Richard Lipkin, "Risky Business of Assessing Danger," *Insight* (May 23, 1988), 8–13.

19. See "Water Pollution, Pesticide Residues, and Cancer," *Water*, vol. 27, no. 2 (Summer 1986), 23–24, adapted from Bruce Ames' testimony.

20. Ibid, 23. Also see Bruce N. Ames, Renae Magan, and Lois Swirsky Gold, "Ranking Possible Carcinogenic Hazards," *Science*, vol. 236 (April 17, 1987), 271–80.

21. U.S. Environmental Protection Agency, "Unfinished Business: A Comparative Assessment of Environmental Problems: Overview Report" (Washington: U.S. Environmental Protection Agency, February 1987).

22. See Survey and Investigations Staff, "A Report to the Committee on Appropriations, U.S. House of Representatives, on the Status of the Environmental Protection Agency's Superfund Program" (March 1988).

23. Paul R. Portney, "Reforming Environmental Regulation: Three Modest Proposals," *Issues in Science and Technology*, vol. IV, no. 2 (Winter 1988), 74–81.

24. See Harold C. Barnett, "The Allocation of Superfund, 1981-1983," *Land Economics*, vol. 61, no. 3 (August 1985), 255–62.

25. See Douglas W. McNeil, Andrew W. Foshee, and Clark R. Burbee, "Superfund Taxes and Expenditures: Regional Redistribution," *Review of Regional Studies*, vol. 18, no. 1 (Winter 1988), 4–9.

7

Effects of the
Environmental Saga

INTRODUCTION

Meeting the requirements of the regulatory maze spawned
by legislation of the 1970s and 1980s required massive expenditures by the targeted industries. The associated design,
installation, and operation of pollution control equipment that
accompanied the technology-based regulation was a major part
of the response. Unfortunately, we know more about the extent
and cost of that activity than of those actions involving the relocation of people and plants, the alteration of product and process designs, the hiring of additional management to deal with
and affect the regulatory process, and the social burden imposed when older, less effective products were not replaced by
newer, more effective ones because of the burden of regulation.
Regulation induced higher levels of action in these non-capital-
using activities, and these along with all other operating costs
ultimately hit the pocket of consumers and industries' bottom
line.

The share of all new capital investment accounted for by
investment in pollution control capital for major industries
for the years 1975 through planned 1987 is shown in Table 3, which illustrates one dimension of the change that
occurred. As indicated, the primary metal industry, which
included steelmaking, made major capital commitments early in the saga, with 17.2 percent of all new 1975 capital going

Table 3
Pollution Control Expenditures as a Share of Total Capital Expenditures, 1975–1987

Industry	1975	1980	1981	1985	1987
Primary Metals	17.2	12.7	9.6	11.5	7.7
Fabricated Metals	NA	2.4	2.4	2.2	1.7
Electric Machinery	5.8	1.7	1.7	1.2	1.4
Other Machinery	1.8	1.7	1.1	1.0	0.8
Motor Vehicles	3.9	4.3	3.5	3.8	5.1
Aircraft	2.4	1.4	1.6	0.9	1.5
Stone, Clay, Glass	14.3	6.5	5.1	3.8	5.1
Food	5.2	3.7	3.6	2.4	2.3
Textiles	4.6	4.3	3.2	1.7	2.8
Paper	16.8	5.7	5.7	6.8	7.8
Chemicals	10.9	5.8	6.4	4.5	6.2
Petroleum	11.8	8.3	5.6	4.7	7.7
Rubber	4.0	1.7	2.3	2.1	1.9
Mining	2.0	3.6	2.7	2.0	1.9
Electric Utilities	9.7	10.0	10.0	7.7	5.3

Source: Data for 1975 and 1980, Tom Tietenberg, *Environmental and Natural Resource Economics*, Glenview, Illinois: Scott, Foresman and Company, 1988, p. 459. Other data are from *Survey of Current Business*, various issues. Share calculated by dividing total pollution control capital expenditures into total capital expenditures. Data for 1987 are planned expenditures.

to pollution control. After 1975 that industry's share declined. Similar large hits are seen for the stone, clay and glass; pulp and paper; chemical; and petroleum industries.

In some cases, the described capital commitment was related primarily to air pollution control, which is perhaps the most costly of all pollution control problems. In other cases, the chief problem was water pollution. But in every case, the capital devoted to pollution control was intended to produce a new good—environmental quality, which, although highly valued by the American people, was a product that did not reflect new revenues and profits in the affected firms' operating statements.

While these highly visible and more readily measured costs are massive, they may be smaller than the invisible costs of environmental control, the losses that spring from reduced production, lost productivity, and misallocated resources. One policy analyst suggested that the tightest of all air pollution standards would impose the lowest costs. At some point, he reasoned, the affected industry would simply disappear. After that, there would be no recorded costs to worry about, and the air would be cleaner. Although no report card is maintained on losses that spring from disappearing industries, if that happened to all producers, invisible costs would become highly visible.

A related thought experiment asks us to think about efforts to design and market a new chemical product that will supplant an older, perhaps riskier product, as environmental regulations become tougher. The tighter and more costly the regulatory screening process, the more difficult becomes the entry process. At some point, the expected improvements in revenues and profits associated with the new product will not jump the cost hurdle. The older product continues in the market. What losses will we find when data are examined? Only the nonproductive research and development expenditures that failed to produce a better product. Again, invisible costs can be much more important than visible ones.

Trying to corral all costs and determine their magnitude is obviously an impossible challenge. But what might have been in the absence of federal efforts to improve the environment is the appropriate benchmark to set when trying to evaluate what actually happened. The difficulties encountered when seeking that pre-federal baseline sometimes force analysts to focus on the economic effects of EPA's program. However, the fact that states and local governments would have been doing something and that industry would have been taking actions to control pollution must be remembered when such studies are evaluated.

PRODUCTIVITY EFFECTS

Edward Denison was one of the first analysts to perform a systematic analysis of the overall effects of major regulations on the performance of the national economy.[1] Denison examined the period 1948 to 1973 and found that environmental and safety and health regulation contributed about 20 percent of the two percentage-point decline in productivity that occurred in that period. Later, Gregory B. Christensen and Robert H.

Haveman focused on productivity growth between 1947 and 1982 and used three measures of the intensity of regulation: 1) the total number of pieces of major regulation in effect each year, 2) the total number of workers employed in the regulation agencies, and 3) the level of real expenditures budgeted for the various agencies.[2]

Christensen and Haveman found little regulatory effect until the mid-1960s, a time that also marks the origin of major environmental legislation. At that point, productivity growth began to decline, and the diminution was led by expenditures by regulatory agencies. The authors found that regulation had practically zero effect from 1958 to 1965, a negative effect on productivity gains of from 0.1 to 0.3 percentage points during 1965 to 1973, and imposed a loss of from 0.2 to 0.3 percentage points during 1973 to 1977. Those losses accounted for about 15 percent of the overall slowdown in labor productivity in 1973 to 1977 relative to 1958 to 1965.

More recently, Wayne Gray has made estimates and surveyed other studies of the impact of EPA and OSHA regulations for 450 manufacturing industries across the years 1960 to 1980.[3] Gray's initial review of the data focused on two commonly used measures of productivity—the change in output per worker, commonly called labor productivity, and the change in output relative to all inputs used by industries. Labor productivity had been rising at almost 3 percent annually in the late 1950s and early 1960s. That growth rate fell sharply, hitting 1.5 percent in 1973–78 and 0.86 percent in 1973–80. At the same time, the stock of pollution control capital grew at a much larger rate than the total capital stock.

Gray's statistical work revealed that regulation—the combined effects of enforcement, capital investment, and operating costs—accounted for 39 percent of the loss in productivity in the 1970s, with OSHA and EPA sharing equally in the loss. Trying to dislodge the findings, in the tradition of doing good scientific work, Gray introduced the effects of energy shocks and a generally slow economy. The noted regulatory effects survived.

But what does a 39 percent loss of productivity mean? Worker earnings rise with productivity and decline when productivity falls. In 1970 the average worker in manufacturing earned

$134 each week. In 1980, a similar worker received $129 (in 1970 dollars). Had the loss in productivity attributed to environmental and safety and health regulation not occurred, and if the average worker wages had recovered that amount, the 1980 paycheck would have been $164, again in 1970 dollars. The $35 difference in weekly earnings may appear small to some, but when multiplied by 20 million workers in manufacturing, the number becomes a rather respectable $700 million each week (stated in 1970 dollars). That's $36 billion in annual consumer buying and taxpaying power, which stated in current dollars amounts to better than $90 billion. According to Gray's estimate, half of that was associated with efforts to control pollution.

It must be recognized that extrapolations of this kind are hazardous. Aside from the environmental saga, many other things changed in the decade of the 1970s. However, even if the projections are halved, the effects on worker earnings and family income loom large. Still, there are other important cost elements to consider.

A 1984 EPA report on the cost of clean air and water indicates that the government's program of managing air for the 1970s cost $9.3 billion (1981 dollars).[4] The report projected the next decade's management costs would run about $5 billion.

Industry costs of $90 billion for installing air pollution control devices in the 1970s forms another dimension to the story, a dimension that is captured in the productivity studies. And the cost of installing pollution control equipment on automobiles adds another $72 billion to the decade's tally. With billions spent on equipment, regulatory activities, and with billions in lost earnings, other major effects had to show up somewhere in the economy.

EFFECTS ON REGIONAL DEVELOPMENT

Capital expenditures of the sort generated by EPA's water and air pollution control programs cannot occur without affecting the number and kinds of plants built. Environment intensive industries are placed at a disadvantage relative to other economic activity, which is the expected effect when actions are taken to reduce pollution. But there are differential effects within the affected industries. Economies of size associated with waste removal and working through the regulatory maze favor larger firms and plants. Enforcement of rules that favor some regions of the country over others is by design destined to alter development patterns. Legislation that provides subsidies for the treatment of waste in publicly owned treatment works benefits firms near cities, which penalizes those in remote locations. Rules that reduce opportunities for the production of new chemical insecticides, medicines, photographic materials, and that raise the cost of working with toxic materials will obviously bias the economic growth of regions where those activities are located.

A number of studies confirm these theory-based statements. Environmental regulation has been shown to impose higher costs on smaller firms, to alter patterns of economic development in the United States, to affect the location of water-using industries, and to alter the economic fortunes of people who live in their host regions.[5] Again, there are studies that reveal interesting differential effects that occurred across firms and industries.

Larger enterprises, which might otherwise gain a cost advantage from scale economies, are lower cost targets for enforcing regulation, which means smaller enterprises escape part of the burden imposed by the rules. Large integrated steel makers, electric utilities, mining and smelter operations, and other massive industrial plants that have highly specialized, site-specific capital, tend to stay under the regulatory magnifying glass. Since those industries lack the locational flexibility of other industries, their production cannot be relocated to other points on the globe. Moving to friendlier locations is out of the question.

While the grind of international competition can eventually take its toll on site-bound domestic industries that face higher environmental costs, ultimately replacing domestic production with foreign-made goods, that process cannot work directly for the production of electricity. The electric utilities have geographic franchises, a duty to serve a defined market, and because of these substantial legal and economic barriers cannot consider relocating production. Of course, the production of goods that require large amounts of electricity in their manufacturing process can be relocated, but residential users tend to remain in place.

Along with these locational rigidities, electric utilities are unlike other major industries in another important respect. The prices they charge are regulated. Strict pollution control regulation that requires new capital and higher operating costs can be embodied in requests for higher rates. With their monopoly status and flexibility in pricing, we would expect the utilities to be sitting ducks for heavy regulation. We should also expect to see less efficient regulation applied to that industry, since competitive pressures that might influence the regulators to consider lower cost alternatives are much weaker. In a way, the data in Table 3 reflects all this. While the share of capital devoted to environmental control for most major industries fell after a few years of heavy expenditures, the share for utilities continued at a relatively high and constant pace.

IMPACT ON INDUSTRIAL EXPANSION

One of the most rigorous studies undertaken to measure the effect of air pollution on manufacturing was reported in 1984 by Peter Pashigian.[6] Pashigian focused on the regulation of emissions from 319 manufacturing industries and studied data for the period 1958 through 1977. His estimates of the impact of the Clean Air Act across the noted period show a 12 percent reduction in plants for the 319 industries. Looking closer at the 20 most affected industries, Pashigian found that 400 plants "did not exist in those 20 industries because of environmental regulation."[7]

Going further in his work, Pashigian found emission regulation had a significant and strong effect on smaller plants.

Once again, the outcome was regressive. Even with the "sitting duck" phenomenon described earlier, which seems to work against larger plants, smaller plants were penalized disproportionately.

In a 1983 study, I searched for regional effects that might be related to pollution regulation.[8] Using data for 1953 through 1977, I focused on the growth in value added in manufacturing across the fifty states. To make the linkage to pollution control effects, I used the share of employment accounted for by the five industries that invested the greatest share of capital in pollution control equipment, using data like that presented in Table 3. Those were primary metals; stone, clay and glass; pulp and paper; chemical; and petroleum. I did not include electric utilities since they cannot easily relocate, and relative growth and relocation effects were central issues in the study.

The tabulation of the data on those two variables revealed a pattern. The states with the highest share of pollution capital showed the slowest growth in value added in manufacturing. The statistical modeling conducted in the research sup ported the relationship, after taking into account wage rates, fuel costs, taxes, and other variables that might affect industrial growth across the states.

The slower growth effect detected was present in 1963–67, 1967–72, and in 1972–77, and its magnitude rose through time. Environmental variables included in the study, such as population density and the amount of nonurban space, became more binding as the statistical tests progressed into the 1970s. The results indicate that as environmental regulation became stricter, especially so for new plants, locations in rural areas became more attractive. Populous states with heavy concentrations of polluting industries were placed at a disadvantage by the implementation of the federal programs. Of course, that was before the invention of the rules having to do with prevention of significant deterioration, which arrived in 1977.

THE EFFECTS ON CONSUMERS

Consumers and citizens ultimately pay all economic costs, either in the prices paid for products, higher taxes, or the loss of goods no longer produced. And given the nature of the regulatory process, the overall burden falls heaviest on the poor.[9] To illustrate, 1980 environmental costs were estimated to range from 4.90 to 5.42 percent of family income for those earning $3,500 annually or less. Those costs average about 1.4 percent of family income for those in the $35,600 to $46,200 income bracket. The burden becomes increasingly smaller as income rises. It is understandable that research findings indicate environmental quality is an income-elastic good.

Baumol and Oates provide a detailed discussion of the linkage between higher incomes and higher demand for government actions to improve environmental quality in one of their major works on the subject.[10] They report strong evidence from surveys and statistical analysis of citizen votes on environmental issues that support the notion that higher-income people are far more interested in and committed to improvements in the environment than are lower-income people. Having earlier discussed the regressive nature of the costs of environmental protection—that lower-income people pay proportionally more for the benefits they receive—Baumol and Oates conclude with the advice for would-be legislators that "this suggests the need to formulate and finance environmental programs in a way that makes them less onerous to lower-income families, both as a matter of social justice *and* as a means to generate support necessary to institute effective environmental measures."[11]

Recognizing that environmental control provides an opportunity for higher-income citizens to receive subsidies from lower-income people is one thing; trying to alter that outcome is something else. Some of the regressive costs hit certain products harder than others. For example, emission controls on automobiles raise the price of all automobiles, both new and old, as the price of autos is bid up. This gives a one-time gain to owners of old cars.[12] Eventually, however, the lower-income family has to buy a newer car, and the books balance at that time. From then on, lower-income people pay a larger share of their income for transportation services than do higher-income people.

Pollution control of stationary sources is also shown to impose a heavier burden on poorer people, since a larger share of their income goes for food, clothing, and other consumer goods. Sadly, at least for poorer people, proportionally more of the benefits of pollution control accrue to higher-income people. Stricter pollution controls are forced on industries that affect rich neighborhoods more than poor neighborhoods. Industrial waste sites and landfills are more frequently located "across the track," and priorities for cleaning them tend to follow higher–income people. Furthermore, while urban air may be cleaner today than in 1960, there are greater concentrations of poorer people in cities, which means average exposure to pollution is still higher for poor people.

What About the Benefits?

Whether paid by poor or rich people, the expenditures for environmental quality have been massive. The total measurable cost of controls paid by the industrial sector for air pollution control in the 1970s hit $90 billion.[13] The measured cost of regulating mobile sources comes in with an almost matching $79 billion. Estimates for the 1980s put the manufacturing sector's share at $170 billion, of which $95 billion will be incurred by public utilities. From 1970 through 1990, some $14 billion is expected to be spent in operating the state-local-federal regulatory apparatus.

With such massive expenditures and evidence of effects across industries, regions, and consumers, we should expect to see significant changes for the better in environmental quality. At the outset, however, we should recognize that it takes time to generate changes in air and water quality. There is an understandable lag between capital investment and changes in environmental quality.

What about the benefits? What does the record say? Can measured improvements in overall air and water quality be attributed to EPA's major programs? Or have those programs simply continued the progress that was being made by state and local governments in the pre-federal period?

These questions are difficult to answer, for one cannot simply examine current levels of emissions and effluent and make an accurate judgment. For example, a 1988 Department of Energy report tells the reader that sulfur oxide emissions have fallen since 1970 and are now close to the 1960 level when far less sulfur bearing fuel was being burned.[14] The levels of suspended particulates and gases that affect the ozone layer and lead to smog have fallen since 1970, but the level of nitrogen oxide emissions rose after 1970 and plateaued at a slightly higher level. These data are also reflected in reports from the Council on Environmental Quality and The Conservation Foundation.

We also observe improvements in water quality for some lakes and major rivers, especially those located near major cities. But there are other reports on water quality that suggest no progress has been made since 1970, which may still represent an accomplishment of sorts.[15]

But as good or as bad as the data might be, the data alone cannot answer the question. The problem is much like one encountered when examining highway safety efforts and the annual number of recorded fatalities. In that case, we must adjust for other things that contribute to fatalities, such as the number of drivers in the 16–25 age category, alcohol consumption, average highway speed, and traffic patterns. In the case of environmental quality, we must adjust for levels of economic activity, changes in industry mix, alterations in fuel consumption, and anything else that makes a difference in observed environmental quality. As described by the Conservation Foundation when addressing this same problem:

Explaining why changes occur in monitored ambient concentrations or estimated emissions is even more problematic. Year-to-year improvement or deterioration in air quality occurs for a number of reasons aside from the presence or absence of pollution control efforts. Some major sources of pollution may have closed or moved elsewhere, decreasing pollution levels at their old site and increasing levels at their new one. Temporary economic slowdowns may have caused an equally temporary reduction in industrial emissions. Or climatic conditions may have changed for better or worse.[16]

Even if all these adjustments could be made, serious attention would have to be focused on the data used for measuring environmental quality before embarking on a heavy-duty research project. Sadly, the data on emissions, water quality, and air quality are in some cases inaccurate, in others inconsistent across time, and in yet other instances, do not reflect conditions where it is important to do so.

According to the Conservation Foundation, EPA sometimes changes the underlying assumptions used in making calculations for data reported to the public.[17] The foundation reports that EPA's 1980 emission trend estimate showed only a slight decline in air pollution across the years 1970 to 1978. The agency's 1982 report showed a substantial decline in emissions for the same years. As it turns out, there is questionable evidence that the overall air quality in large American cities has improved significantly in the last decade.[18]

The problem with the air quality monitoring system was raised in a 1978 General Accounting Office report, which stated that the extent of polluter compliance with the laws was simply unknown.[19] At the time, the audit agency noted that, "Billions of dollars have been spent on air pollution controls, and since the Clean Air Act was passed in 1970, some progress has been made in cleaning the nation's air . . . . The Environmental Protection Agency's efforts to enforce the Clean Air Act, however, could have been more effective. Its efforts have been mostly administrative with almost no legal action. Consequently, violators have not taken corrective action."

After auditing EPA's performance in one region, the GAO found that 70 percent of the emission sources subject to EPA enforcement action in 1973 five years later were still not in compliance with the law. In another region, 321 major sources of pollution were not in compliance at the end of 1977, and no action had been taken against half the firms.

GAO went on to condemn EPA's poor efforts to monitor and report emission levels. They noted that EPA had reported 92 percent of the major emission sources in the United States were in compliance, but that GAO found no data that accurately indicated the status of compliance for the 23,000 major sources of pollution in the United States. The report suggested EPA's actions and the environmental saga were more symbolic than real, at least at the end of 1977.

The monitoring data problem cited by GAO in 1978 did not go away. In fact, the agency addressed the issue again in 1982, and the Conservation Foundation emphasized the problem repeatedly in its 1987 report that focuses on the state of the environment.[20]

Unfortunately for those who really care about progress toward achieving important goals of environmental quality, reliable data on water pollution appears to be as weak as that for air pollution. There is no consistent set of monitors, no common set of pollutants observed across monitors, and no way to systematically evaluate the data. Indeed, the GAO has been as critical of those data as for air pollution data.[21]

In spite of these problems, which are certainly indicative of political pressures EPA faces when attempting to enforce difficult statutes, there is persuasive evidence that some important dimensions of the environment have improved. But had EPA done nothing, the same result might have obtained, thanks partly to the energy crisis. America's industrial structure and consumption patterns changed significantly with the rapid increase in energy prices, the inflation that followed, and the economic slowdown that came later. Pollution obviously declines with output.

All of the empirical work that attempts to adjust for these effects while searching for improvements generated by federal regulation has shortcomings, not the least of which is the monitoring data used in them. But to the study, all of them raise serious questions as to whether federal regulation made a dent in the problem. A 1979 study by Paul MacAvoy was one of the first such efforts.[22] At the outset of the work, MacAvoy noted that, "Total emissions were reduced substantially in the early 1970s for only two of six major air pollutants—particulates and carbon monoxide—and slightly for two more—hydrocarbons and sulfur dioxide. Emissions of nitrogen oxides increased in this period, although at a slower rate than in previous periods."[23]

MacAvoy expresses doubt, however, that EPA contributed to the few improvements he found in his study. Examining industry trends for 1968–1976 and adjusting for capacity utilization and the presence of EPA regulation, he found EPA fostered increases in pollution from automobiles and electric utilities, but found no improvements at the industry level that could be attributed to EPA's presence.

Lester B. Lave and Gilbert S. Omenn completed another assessment of activities under the Clean Air Act and reported their findings in 1981.[24] After reviewing the history of efforts to reduce air emissions nationwide, and recognizing that progress had been made in a number of local situations, Lave and Omenn looked for overall net benefits and concluded:

The current system of abatement of air pollution in the United States is in trouble. While regulations have reduced emissions from new plants and vehicles, virtually all the abatement of pollution from existing sources has resulted from switching to cleaner fuels. The Clean Air Act of 1963 and subsequent amendments set lofty goals and compelled the attention of polluters, but they have not brought forth effective and efficient abatement of air pollution. Implementation requires more than goals and rhetoric; it must tie together complex aspects of physics, chemistry, public health, engineering, economics, politics, and social values under the pressure of firm, enforceable deadlines.[25]

Of course, the assessment sounded good, but the problem described at the end was no simple matter, certainly not for EPA and the political economy that drives and alters the agency's actions.

Going on with the discussion, the two authors indicate that "coal use has been the dominant factor influencing air quality for hundreds of years and will remain so for the decade ahead."[26] Suggesting that all that EPA might do made little difference, barring major changes in fuel use, hardly offered comfort to consumers and investors who had spent billions on higher-priced goods and pollution control machinery.

Robert W. Crandall's assessment of EPA's record was reported in 1983.[27] Using both earlier and more recent data than that used by MacAvoy, and emphasizing the crude nature of the data themselves, Crandall reported, "Every tabulation since 1972 shows less relative improvement than was achieved in the 1960s. Sulfur dioxide concentration appears to have fallen

11.3 percent per year from 1964 through 1971 but no more than 4.6 percent per year in the 1970s. Similarly, the average concentration of TSP (total suspended particulates) fell 2.3 percent per year in the 1960–71 period, but only 0.6 percent per year from 1972 to 1980." While that part of his conclusion is discouraging enough, Crandall's final thought drove a proverbial nail in the casket. "Therefore, these data suggest that pollution reduction was more effective in the 1960s before there was a serious federal policy dealing with stationary sources, than since the 1970 Clean Air Amendments."

What Does the Absence of Good Data Mean?

In the light of these studies and the data difficulties encountered by those who seek to understand just what is going on, what can we conclude? The fact that after almost twenty years there is no consistent set of data that tracks environmental quality for the entire country that can survive close scrutiny supports either of two hypotheses about the situation. The first states that the American scientific community is incapable of developing a monitoring system or that the cost of doing so is prohibitive. That, of course, is hogwash. The magnitude of resources committed and spent on environmental control suggest that the comparative cost of improving monitoring capabilities would look like a shoelace next to the Washington Monument. And the hypothetical argument that technical capacity is lacking to build monitors flies in the face of the pollution control strategy that has been followed from the outset of the saga. The control strategies themselves rely on the ability to measure the pre-control and post-control effects. Put simply, we would have no way of determining which plants and places to control if we could not measure what is going on.

The second hypothesis, which appears to be the more reliable one, argues that we have the knowledge and ability to build monitors and track data, but that we assign little value to doing so. Those who are interested in knowing about environmental trends apparently lack the political muscle to get that information. This suggests rather paradoxically that the community of interests that delivered federal environmental regulation in the first place and continues to support those institutions is not particularly interested in getting a report card. Why might that be so?

Speculating on that question suggests several things. First, it is perhaps not very important to large national environmental organizations to focus on overall effects, what is happening to the nation. Members of the National Wildlife Federation, Friends of the Earth, the Sierra Club, and other such organizations are understandably more interested in local or regional issues that have common features that bind the group's national programs. The Clean Air Act offers a mechanism for reducing pollution everywhere, but most people are interested in reducing pollution somewhere, usually in their local environment. We would not expect to see a large contingency of environmentalists from South Carolina at a California rally. But we would expect to see the two groups convening to discuss a national legislative strategy. In other words, there is no such thing as a broad public interest; there are collections of narrow special interests that share a common bond.

A second thought relates to EPA itself, the politically managed vehicle that partly serves the interests of the environmental coalitions. To some degree, the creation of EPA was a response to political pressures orchestrated by environmental organizations on their way to becoming national organizations. As Paul Downing describes the history of the movement, the Sierra Club, founded in 1892, enjoyed a membership of 15,000 members in the 1960s, and most of those were Californians.[28] By 1970, after successful lobbying and the passage of federal legislation, the group had 107,000 members, a number that rose to 180,000 seven years later. Friends of the Earth, a spin-off from the Sierra Club, was formed in 1969, just as the federal period was beginning. The Center for Law in the Public Interest was organized in 1971, the Environmental Defense Fund in 1967, and the Natural Resources Defense Council in 1969.

These and other environmental groups were instrumental in organizing EPA, and their members received special positions within the agency. The agency has responded by providing taxpayer money to support the growth and activities of the organizations. In the 1970s and 1980s, Congress transferred $915,000 of taxpayer money to the National Wildlife Federation, $790,000 to the Sierra Club, and $1,309,000 to the Center for Renewable Resources.[29] Another $3,828,000 went to the National Center for Appropriate Technologies, and more than a million in taxpayer funds was granted to the Natural Resources Defense Council.

While documenting taxpayer support for environmentalists that are sometimes funneled through EPA, Bennett and Dilorenzo also describe what happened in 1981, and 1982 when EPA Administrator Anne Burford closed the money valves.[30] The Natural Resource Defense Fund had received from EPA $360,000 in 1980 and $816,000 in January 1981. The funding was cut to $178 after Burford took office. The National Wildlife Federation's EPA support was cut from $498,000 in 1981 to one-fourth that amount. Other important environmental groups were cut off entirely. The strong supporters of the agency, those that had been instrumental in its founding, were understandably outraged by the sad turn of events.

All this suggests that environmental groups, which draw their support nationally and use the federal bureaucracy as a support device for such endeavors, really serve narrow interests. At the margin of budgetary growth, we should not expect them to be highly critical of EPA's monitoring, constantly badgering the agency to develop a better national report card. To the contrary, we would predict those groups to seek their narrow interests—always urging an expansion of programs and stricter enforcement of laws that limit industrial pollution, and identifying new environmental hazards that deserve attention. All those activities promote the environmental cause, fuel revenues to the organizations, and provide strength to EPA's position.

Since we cannot expect support for an environmental report card from environmentalists, it is unlikely one will emerge. The diverse citizenry who bear the costs of environmental control are not likely to be aware of thirty-year trends. They are aware of current conditions and announcements of new life-threatening hazards. They obviously want action on current problems, as they perceive them. Whatever EPA has done in the past, more should be done in the future. Why worry about a report card when aquifers and water supplies are being threatened. In other words, ordinary people are rationally ignorant about EPA's overall performance.

The coalition of emitters—the industrial sector—is generally fighting today's battles. Pragmatic as they should be, industry leaders have little to gain by agitating for an environmental report card. Such information might be important if the premise of federal regulation were being questioned, but this is a highly unlikely circumstance.

The political economy of accurate national data on environmental progress suggests we should be grateful for what we have, yet hopeful that marginal improvements will be made in the collection and treatment of that data. Progress will be made, but advances will be slow, ponderous, and perhaps accidental outcomes that spring from somewhat unrelated efforts.

FINAL THOUGHTS

Throughout the work by academics and policy analysts on environmental issues, one finds a constant theme regarding benefits and costs. Costs can be estimated with much greater ease than benefits. The discussion here suggests that neither category of effects can be estimated with precision, but that there are greater incentives to estimate and report costs than benefits.

The real cost of any endeavor, be it guarding the environment or building houses, is the opportunity lost when resources are reallocated to that purpose. We generally accept market determined prices and wages as reflecting the approximate value of the next best alternative.

The price linkages are lost when government action dictates change. Command and control regulation does not compete in the marketplace. Bids are not offered for emission reductions. For that reason and others, we have no way of using market signals to determine what might have been. Capital expenditures on pollution control equipment, the cost of operating the federal bureaucracy, and price effects attributed to environmental control are crude proxies of cost. We know the opportunity cost is large, relative to what could be purchased with those same resource expenditures.

Although we have only a rough approximation of some of the costs of environmental control, we can estimate some of the effects. With considerable confidence, we can argue that industrial structure and locations have been altered. We can tell that some regions have flourished industrially and others have languished. Part of that change can be attributed to environmental regulation.

We are even more confident about the distributional effects of the saga. It is clear that poorer people in general have borne the brunt of the costs of pollution control and have reaped the smaller share of the benefits. In that sense, the saga is something of an elitist movement, something fostered and enjoyed by higher-income people.

With all these effects estimated as best they might be, an examination of the real benefits is equally troublesome, or at least confusing. There are clearly benefits. The air over many major urban centers is cleaner. Major lakes and rivers now sustain aquatic life, and many hazardous dumps have been cleaned. But while a long list of accomplishments can be compiled, we have no way of making overall statements. It is possible for many sites to be made cleaner while a few deteriorate further, leaving all people taken together in a worse condition. There are distributional considerations to be made.

Given the benefits, which are questioned by a number of important analysts, a question remains as to just how much any of this can be attributed to the environmental saga, the massive expenditures, dislocations, and confrontations. The best work, as crude as it is, leaves more than an open question. The work suggests that the rate of improvement has fallen, relative to the pre-federal period, that in some cases, things are worse, not better. In spite of that, however, we know that the world has changed in the last twenty years. The U.S. population has increased; the burning of coal has risen substantially, just to mention one major source of pollution; and the character of the wastes discharged has become more complex. In short, while we can be confident that much more could have been done to improve environmental quality, using the same resources if cost effectiveness had overpowered special interest demands, we will never know what the picture would have been in the absence of the federal period.

NOTES

1. See Edward F. Denison, "Explanations of Declining Productivity Growth," *Survey of Current Business* (August 1979), 1–24.

2. See Gregory B. Christensen and Robert H. Haveman, "The Reagan Administration's Regulatory Relief: A Mid-Term Assessment," in George C. Eads and Michael Fix, eds., *The Reagan Regulatory Strategy: An Assessment* (Washington: Urban Institute Press, 1984), 49–80.

3. See Wayne B. Gray, "The Impact of OSHA and EPA Regulation on Productivity," Working Paper No. 1405 (National Bureau of Economic Research, Inc., July 1984). In his work, Gray reviews the above works by Christensen and Haveman, and Denisen, as well as that of Robert W. Crandall, "Pollution Controls and Productivity Growth in Basic Industries," in Thomas B. Cowing and Rodney E. Stevenson, eds., *Productivity Measurement in Regulated Industries* (New York: Academic Press, 1981); J.R. Northsworthy, Michael J. Harper, and Kent Knuze, "The Slowdown in Productivity Growth: Analysis of Some Contributing Factors," *Brookings Papers on Economic Activity, 1979*, no. 2, 387–421; and F.M Scherer, "Inter-industry Technology Flows and Productivity Growth," *Review of Economics and Statistics*, vol. 64, no. 4 (1982), 627–34.

4. See U.S. Environmental Protection Agency, *The Cost of Clean Air and Water Report to Congress*, 1984, Executive Summary (Washington: U.S. Environmental Protection Agency, May 1984).

5. See Bruce Yandle, "Environmental Control and Regional Growth," *Growth and Change*, vol. 15, no. 3 (July 1984), 39-42; Robert Quinn and Bruce Yandle, "Expenditures on Air Pollution Control Under Federal Regulation," *Review of Regional Studies*, vol. 16, no. 3 (Fall 1986), 11–16; Bruce Yandle, "Economic Agents and the Level of Pollution Control," *Public Choice*, vol. 40 (1983), 105–9; B. Peter Pashigian, "The Effects of Environmental Regulation on Optimal Plant Size and Factor Shares," *Journal of Law and Economics*, vol. 27 (April 1984), 1–28; B. Peter Pashigian, "Environmental Regulation: Whose Interests are Being Protected?" *Economic Inquiry*, vol. 23 (October 1985), 551–84; Robert W. Crandall, *Controlling Industrial*

Pollution (Washington: The Brookings Institution, 1983), 110–30; and Anand Bhansali, Charles Diamond, and Bruce Yandle, "Sewers as Subsidies" (Center for Policy Studies: Clemson University, Clemson, S.C., 1986).

6. See B. Peter Pashigian, "The Effects of Environmental Regulation Optimal Plant Size and Factor Shares," *Journal of Law and Economics*, vol. 27 (April 1984), 1–28.

7. Ibid., 29.

8. See Bruce Yandle, "Regional Effects of Environmental Regulation," *Growth and Change*, vol. 15, no. 3 (July 1984), 39–42.

9. See U.S. Department of Commerce, *Regulatory Reform Seminar* (October 1978), A66–A70. The data on this were provided by the Public Interest Economic Center.

10. See William J. Baumol and Wallace E. Oates, *Economics, Environmental Policy, and the Quality of Life* (Englewood Cliffs, N.J.: Prentice-Hall, Inc., 1979), esp. 174–89.

11. Ibid., 187.

12. This discussion is based on Tom Tietenberg, *Environmental and Natural Resource Economics* (Glenview, Ill.: Scott, Foresman and Company, 1988), 456–76.

13. See U.S. Environmental Protection Agency, *The Cost of Clean Air and Water Report to Congress, 1984*, Executive Summary (Washington: U.S. Environmental Protection Agency, May 1984).

14. See U.S. Department of Energy, *United States Energy Policy, 1980–1988* (Washington: U.S. Department of Energy, October 1988), 152.

15. See Helen M. Ingram and Dean E. Mann, "Preserving the Clean Water Act: The Appearance of Environmental Victory," *Environmental Policy in the 1980s: Reagan's New Agenda*, Norman J. Vig and Michael E. Kraft, eds. (Washington: Congressional Quarterly Press, 1984).

16. See The Conservation Foundation, *State of the Environment: A View Toward the Nineties* (Washington: The Conservation Foundation, 1987), 57.

17. The Conservation Foundation, *State of the Environment: 1982* (Washington: The Conservation Foundation, 1982), 50.

18. See The Conservation Foundation, *State of the Environment: An Assessment at Mid-Decade* (Washington: The Conservation Foundation, 1984), 86–105.

19. U.S. General Accounting Office, *Improvements Needed in Controlling Major Air Pollution Sources* (Washington: General Accounting Office, 1978), i.

20. For a summary of the later GAO report and the full discussion, see The Conservation Foundation, *State of the Environment: A View Toward the Nineties* (Washington: The Conservation Foundation, 1987), 54–116.

21. Ibid., 88.

22. Paul W. MacAvoy, *The Regulated Industries and the Economy* (New York: W.W. Norton & Company, 1979), 94–104.

23. Ibid., 101.

24. Lester B. Lave and Gilbert S. Omenn, *Cleaning the Air: Reforming the Clean Air Act* (Washington: The Brookings Institution, 1981).

25. Ibid., 44.

26. Ibid.

27. Robert W. Crandall, *Controlling Industrial Pollution: The Economics and Politics of Clean Air* (Washington: The Brookings Institution, 1983).

28. Paul B. Downing, *Environmental Economics and Policy* (Boston: Little, Brown and Company, 1984), 263–68.

29. See James T. Bennett and Thomas J. Dilorenzo, *Destroying Democracy: How Government Funds Partisan Politics* (Washington: Cato Institute, 1985), 137–72.

30. Ibid., 159–60.

8

There Are Political Limits to Environmental Quality Regulation

LESSONS FROM THE SAGA

We have now examined major and minor episodes of the two-decade-long federal effort to manage and improve environmental quality. We started with an interest group theory of government that was intended to illuminate action by intertwined groups who worked America's political economy. The theory of bootleggers and Baptists, described in Chapter 2, argued that at least two strong interest groups are necessary to secure important government favors. One of the groups uses powerful rhetoric about socially important issues and inspires broad support of causes that often take on crisis proportions. The discussions of Love Canal, control of hazardous wastes, and EPA's Superfund program in Chapter 6 are perhaps the most vivid illustrations of crisis building power.

With environmental groups forming the necessary engine of the special interest train, other interest groups hitch their cars and in some cases add another engine to pull the train faster. Segments of industries, labor unions, and local politicians are some of the power groups that join the environmentalists' struggle. These are all candidates for the other necessary interest group in the bootleggers and Baptists theory.

While environmentalists work to secure clear-cut rules that speak to controlling environmental degradation, the others seek that and something of greater importance to them—the delivery of some narrow economic benefits secured by enforcement of environmental regulation. Discussions of the differential treatment of new and old sources of pollution, the policy for the Prevention of Significant Deterioration, and the huge subsidies that came for building municipal treatment works accessed by industry in Chapters 4 and 5 illustrate how strange bedfellows meet regularly in the environmental saga.

Each newly identified pollutant and each new crisis provide opportunities for new political struggles, the stuff that fuels support of all lobby organizations. Each major revision in statutes, each important regulation, and every interpretation of rules that follow lift the importance of the lobby groups and increase opportunities for politicians to draw attention to their own importance. Doing so secures increased support from the many groups drawn to the struggle.

The overwhelming use of command-and-control regulation, as opposed to the implementation of property rights and market incentives, typifies the federal approach to environmental control. Command and control and the accompanying specification of acceptable technologies give power to bureaucrats and congressional staffers and also insure that special interest benefits will be delivered. The efforts by eastern coal miners to secure the specification of scrubbers on newly built power plants, thereby blunting competition of western low sulfur coal, illustrates the importance and political value of command and control. Economic incentives are clearly effective instruments for generating lower-cost control of pollution, but the inevitably higher-cost command-and-control approach always seems to win when the two approaches are debated politically.

Ultimately, as described in Chapter 7, the effects of political competition become highly visible in the economy. At the same time, the recognizable gains in environmental quality are almost invisible. Production costs rise in some industries and in some geographic locations. Some regions prosper relatively while others languish. The burden of environmental control also is shifted across income groups, and almost invariably the heaviest burden falls on the politically weak.

Tales of environmental struggles indicate that the contests themselves sometimes appear to be more important than the end product—an improved environment. The political limits of environmental control suggest final solutions to the problem will never be found, that effective environmental quality regulation is indeed a unicorn. Instead, new crises—some real, others imagined—will emerge regularly. Interest groups will rally around the causes, push for massive legislation, and call for more regulation and larger budgets for regulatory agencies. This seems to be the prediction that comes from a review of the environmental saga.

THE MONOPOLY REGULATOR

Unless carefully qualified, much of the preceding would likely apply to an examination of environmental control in the pre-federal period when individual states and communities worked to find acceptable solutions to pollution problems. For one simple reason, important parts of the discussion could not apply. The move to federal regulation created a monopoly regulator—Congress and the regulatory bodies it authorizes and controls. In the earlier days, if zealous environmentalists in Pittsburgh wanted to clear air and water to the highest possible levels, or if aggressive industrialists sought to flood rivers with more pollution, a serious constraint had to be considered.

Environmental control and environmental use was costly, both in terms of capital outlays and threats to human health. Eventually, hard-pressed citizens moved to other locations that placed different values on health, or on employment and income. The threats to move were disruptive to local political fiefdoms, as well as the local tax base. Political competition sprang up that spanned across many counties, cities, and states.

Federal regulation did not end that competition completely. Instead, the regional battles were transferred to one location—Congress—where differences could be settled by log-rolling and pork barrel politics. Instead of forty-eight or fifty different, independent political bodies making determinations of environmental goals and the means for achieving them, one body did the job. All the pressure groups, lobbyists, and much of the political contributions previously focused on state legislatures and thousands of local governments became concentrated in Washington. Subtle and substantial differences desired by a heterogeneous population were transformed into uniform, homogeneous rules. Once having migrated to the higher levels of government, the prospects were dim for the return of environmental control to local levels.

Concentration of the problem and solution has advantages, certainly to members of Congress and EPA staff, but also to other locomotives that pull the special interest train. Industrialists who are able to secure regulatory certainty across the United States support uniform federal rules. They argue logically that it is efficient to minimize the number of bureaucracies they have to satisfy when developing products and plant sites.

While that is one important reason given for centralizing control, especially for firms and industries that are established and operating, there is another reason for industry to support a federal monopoly regulator. Members of mature industries that assist in the design of regulations at the federal level can have the fine-tuned rules imposed on all their competitors—existing and new. The monopoly regulator can control and limit the entry of new competition across the country.

Politicians at the local and state level who have built constituency support naturally prefer federal regulation. Rules that regulate industrial growth in competing communities and states reduce the likelihood that secure politicians will lose large parts of their support as other economies expand. Along with this important consideration, there are transfers of funds that can be enjoyed by some regions through the generosity of others. Mayors, aldermen, and state senators almost miraculously bring federal dollars to their regions. The monopoly regulator does not lack for their support.

A monopoly regulator has its own peculiar dynamics to consider. Lacking direct competition, the EPA arm of Congress does not need to be overly concerned about cost-effective operations and the on-time delivery of regulatory enforcement actions. As with all monopolies, individuals in the agency no doubt believe they are overworked, underpaid, and dedicated to serving the public interest. They may be. But people in competitive markets feel the same way. The operational difference between the two is found in the subtle, sometimes subconscious, recognition that competition is out there.

To drive the point home, consider American Telephone and Telegraph (AT&T) in its early monopoly days. The firm struggled to expand, provided excellent service, earned only normal profits, and employed hardworking, dedicated employees. Meanwhile, the firm continued to string wire across the country while lower-cost technologies languished. Lacking the spur of competition, the firm could continue its old reliable ways, believing all along that nothing but the best was being provided to consumers in the marketplace. Having nothing with which to compare the bundle of service and price, most consumers agreed.

Monopolists have less reason to inform their customers about their products and services than competitive organizations. The monopolist advertises differently, usually engaging in self-praise. Monopoly regulators have little reason to give definitive report cards about their record of performance. Again, lacking competition, no comparisons can be drawn by customers, and there are no other regulators pointing out weaknesses and failures that might mar the record of an ineffective regulator.

Although there is a veritable avalanche of technical reports published by EPA and occasional public-image reports, the agency understandably offers little public information and time series data about environmental progress that has resulted solely from its efforts. Reports of environmental progress and change are given, but EPA's independent role in that cannot be identified. At the same time, voters seem to ask for little, since they have no other choice but to rely on the monopolist. As with the days of the AT&T long-distance monopoly, the customer seems to be highly satisfied with the product and service, since no informed comparisons can be made, and there is a clear feeling that the producer is doing its very best.

EFFICIENCY SEEKERS AND ENVIRONMEN-TAL REGULATION

The political process that limits environmental control has a place for all interest groups, even those who might be termed efficiency seekers. Some economists and policy analysts earn part of their living and professional recognition from the part they play in the political struggle. Efficiency seekers are often carriers of one of the competing political visions, the one that argues about social costs and benefits, cost effectiveness, the ineffectiveness of command-and-control regulation, and the market process. The higher the public visibility given the environmental struggle and the greater the stakes, the more valuable the efficiency seeker becomes.

Like all others involved in the struggle with the monopoly regulator, efficiency seekers sometimes become caught in the political quicksand. While their work may influence thinking and outcomes so that efficiency gains result, it is also possible that their promptings ensure the continuation of more prosperous days for monopoly regulators. Again, the problem has to do with the interplay of interests, the coalition linkages that form, and the service rendered by experts who may unwittingly serve a particular interest.

The implementation of some of the efficiency seekers' advice requires a strong regulatory presence, the kind provided by a monopoly regulator. For example, EPA's bubble concept provides rich opportunities to reduce the cost of achieving fixed environmental goals, as does the offset mechanism. However, those regulatory approaches have been shoehorned into a complex array of command–and–control regulation. Their use fits the other competing vision discussed in Chapter 1, the unconstrained view that calls for the participation of experts in government who can bring rational direction to an otherwise hopeless process.

Early enthusiasm for bubbles and offsets exhibited by efficiency seekers was partly quenched when the bureaucrats finally unveiled the procedures for implementing them. As indicated in Chapter 4, the bubble concept was allowed for older pollution sources, but not for new. The implied gains strengthened the positions of entrenched industry and established industrial regions.

With the much praised offset mechanism, the ratio of pollution allowed by new sources to that reduced by existing ones is set by state regulators, with EPA approval. That exercise gives political power to state politicians, who may be in a position to extract the maximum political payoff from firms that seek to build new facilities in their region.

None of this is to suggest that efficiency seeking is a waste of time. It is more a warning that such efforts are not immune to the strategic behavior of other interest groups who seek ways to make their positions attractive. There is also a difficult theoretical question to ponder: Can an ineffective regulator be sustained for longer periods by adopting cost-effective, but ineffective, controls?

As pointed out in Chapter 5, EPA's record indicates that an increasingly small amount of overall attention has been given to the use of market-like control devices. At the same time, considerable public attention has been called to those activities. Meanwhile, policy analysts and environmental economists write books and dissertations on the new improved regulatory approaches, but little actual use is made of them.

THE PROSPECT FOR EFFECTIVE CONTROL

There are political limits to environmental control that will always alter outcomes envisioned by those who expect to see gardens blooming in America's necessary waste sites and by those who hope to increase extensive offshore drilling for oil. The limits are real and relate to important political institutions and the level of political competition. That being so, we should ask about the prospects for advancing improvements in the effectiveness of environmental management. Surely, these prospects relate to the possibilities for enhancing the competitiveness of the process.

Under the federal blueprint, competition was expanded across members of Congress. Competition within state and local governing bodies and across political jurisdictions was reduced. Even so, there is a last level of competition that can still discipline a regulator at the national level. There is international competition to consider, and it is very lively.

A monopoly producer of domestic automobiles can act in ways that limit consumer choice so long as the borders are closed to import competition. In the absence of perfect protection, the monopoly producer must be responsive to consumer demand.

The monopoly producer of environmental regulation is in a less secure position than the hypothetical auto producer. High-cost regulation can cause affected producers to expand off-shore. Investors seek higher returns wherever they may be found, and capital moves swiftly. If enough smokestack industries close, the air pollution regulator will have no market. Slower economic growth, lower national income, and loss of job opportunities are the result. The industries, sectors, and regions hardest hit by regulatory costs suffer most. Eventually, the entire economy suffers relative to those of other countries and to the past record.

With mobility of products, investments, and people, relative comparisons can be made at low cost. People become aware that other countries have not all become industrial wastelands, yet they are producing superior products at lower cost. Other more unpleasant outcomes are observed elsewhere. Some countries have allowed for significant environmental deterioration and are taking steps to correct that problem.

International comparisons and competition send messages about the prospects for more effective environmental management. In this sense, Congress and EPA are competing with their counterparts in Canada, Japan, Taiwan, West Germany, the United Kingdom, and elsewhere.

Even that competition can be limited by successful regulatory cartels. Nations that have strong political influence in the international community can attempt to force their environmental rules on trading partners. Compensating tariffs can be imposed on products produced in countries that have different environmental standards and regulations. Since such cartels are never fully successful, the international competition goes on.

Students of environmental regulation are aware of the property rights approach taken in parts of Western Europe and the nonconfrontational nature of environmental control in those countries and in Japan. The struggle there is disciplined strongly by the fact that those economies are heavily export-based. A regulator there cannot destroy or seriously bruise a major exporting industry. Too much economic well-being depends on the export sector. Again, the theme is repeated: There are political limits to environmental control that are formed by the political economy. The expansion of the global economy leaves the United States more exposed and therefore more receptive to ideas that reduce the cost of effective environmental control.

Another stimulus for change in environmental management comes from the deep imprint of environmental regulation on the domestic economy. There are two dimensions to this impulse. The first has to do with the interest groups themselves, the second with the overall cost felt when the effects of manifold rules are registered in the lives of people.

The first effect relates to the original expectations of the interest groups that formed around particular issues. Recall that pure environmentalists are concerned that environmental quality be improved. Others wearing the same cap are described as being against industry and economic development. Then, there are some industrialists who find command-and-control regulation offers an advantage, so long as there are beneficial differential effects registered across new and old firms in the affected industries.

At some point, pure environmentalists recognize that little improvement has come from years of federal control. While there is no way to determine just what might have happened under state regulation, there is a suspicion that things could be better. Not only is command-and-control seen as ineffective, the environmentalists recognize that those opposing their pure position have heavy influence in determining outcomes. They see the political limits to environmental control under the current regime and are ready for change.

The pure environmentalists have no reason to oppose industry for the sake of limiting economic progress. Their opposition has to do with pollution, not production. Seeing that reductions in water and air pollution, for example, are not very large and that industry is being shackled with rules that accomplish less than expected, gives some concern to the purist. There is no point in closing down plants, raising consumer costs, and reducing income if little is gained in exchange. There is some sympathy for industries' position.

The antigrowth or antibusiness lobby, which parades under the banner of environmentalism, faces a difficult problem. The antibusiness objective is obtained with costly but ineffective regulation, but the environmentalist's banner is apt to be pulled away. When true environmentalists argue for new approaches, such as property rights and markets for pollution control, they leave the false environmentalists in the cold. The old coalition of intertwined interests begins to unravel. Although the popularity of being antibusiness rises and falls, people today concerned about international competition, employment growth, and future income are less inclined to support the antibusiness lobby.

Then, there are the industrialists, labor unions, and politicians who have seen EPA rules as a way to delay corrosive economic change and limit future movement of industries from their jurisdictions. Their positions are obviously not frozen in stone. Today's rapid rate of technological change has significant effects in one decade, let alone two.

Because of the toll of time and change on plants and production techniques, some industries that were old and established at the beginning of the environmental saga become a part of the new source problem. Concerns about maintaining their protected positions are replaced by concerns about building new plants and gaining approval of new technologies. Those who supported command-and-control regulation for the sake of uniform certainty and perhaps limiting new competition find they are the new competition. Flexible rules, market incentives, and property rights begin to look far more reasonable to the producer who is attempting to survive in a competitive global economy.

The second dimension of reform support that comes from the all-pervading costs of environmental control is described by Mancur Olson in his intriguing book, *The Rise and Decline of Nations*.[1] Olson describes politically motivated special interest struggles as being typical of human affairs worldwide. Not focusing especially on environmental control or any particular kind of regulation for that matter, Olson's thesis states that all forms of government, be they democracies or dictatorships, are subject and responsive to the tug and pull of special interests.

In their youthful years, societies tend to be more dynamic, still fueled by a pioneer spirit that led to their founding. Issues other than what government can or cannot do overpower the concerns of people. At some point in the maturation process, special interest groups see opportunities to use the machinery of government to protect and enhance wealth positions secured in earlier years. That point comes when the returns from working the halls of government are found to be higher than those obtained from working new capital in manufacturing or farming.

One by one, special interest groups become successful in setting rules that diminish competition. The effect on overall wealth is minimal at first when the protected sectors are small relative to the total economy. But little by little, hardening of arteries sets in. Flexibility is lost as monopoly replaces competition. Eventually, the regulated society ceases to grow, weighted down by regulations.

According to Olson, once regulation becomes all-encompassing, its usefulness ends. All major groups of the regulated society begin to recognize that each group can gain if the regulatory blanket is removed. That leads to a day when sharp deregulation occurs. Alternately, wars, revolutions, and severe natural shocks can so shake a society that dominant special interest groups lose their grips on government. That too leads to new periods of vigorous, less regulated growth.

On occasions, elements of America's environmental saga have reached the point of regulatory relief. The auto industry is an example. With the arrival of the Reagan Administration in 1981, regulators were instructed to give the industry some breathing room. Hit hard by international competition, the industry faced costly fuel economy and emission standards that were legally bound to become even tighter. Regulations were revised and removed, with political support coming from industry, labor unions, and the politicians from the industry's home base. It is difficult for a dying industry to provide much in the way of political support. It is also difficult for environmentalists to control the destiny of auto producers in foreign countries. To have an effect on an industry, there must be a viable industry to affect.

Although environmental regulation is all-encompassing, which is a natural characteristic of federal rules, it is not clear that the burden has been recognized to the extent to cause an Olson-type revision. The prosperous years of the 1980s have countered the burdensome years of the 1970s. Smokestack industries have declined during that time, and new lighter industry and services sectors have brought new environmental challenges that tend to divert attention away from the old ones having to do with such industries as steel and copper.

There is another story to consider, before dismissing the prospect of change that might be generated by all-encompassing environmental regulation. California's Proposition 65, discussed in Chapter 5, is perhaps sufficiently extreme to trigger a reaction. Since West Coast political actions tend to predict future national ones, it seems safe to say that federal rules patterned after California's may soon arrive. When environmental rules become so extensive that they cease to communicate logical information and no longer condition reasonable human action, the nation may be on the path to a revolution in rulemaking. However, before reaching that conclusion, there is more to consider.

True regulatory reform that would itself be all-encompassing is not likely to come until the nation experiences deep recession or a period of very slow growth. All-encompassing change requires congressional action, and there are costly institutional barriers that limit the politicians' behavior. There are political limits to regulatory change, just as there are limits to regulatory control.

The Congressional Limits

In all the discussion of revised interest group positions that come when costs and benefits are finally recognized, all but the position of the federal regulator were mentioned. Of course, politicians do respond to interest group pressures. After all, that is the central theme of this book. But there are lags and there are costs encountered along the way.

Congress is organized along committee lines, and there is no one committee that focuses on environmental control. There are dozens of such committees. Each committee chairman and key committee member worked long and hard to secure his position. It is unlikely that all sectors of society represented by the many committees would simultaneously recognize the overwhelming burden of environmental regulation. The reason is simple; the burden of regulation falls unevenly across the many sectors included in the congressional system.

Instead, the recognition will come in waves, and the waves of reform will come from the various committees. There is no central political intelligence system that gathers all stimuli and responds collectively to them. The response tends to come piecemeal, as with the case of relief for the auto industry.

At times, however, congressional leadership recognizes that some problems are irreconcilable, which is to say the problem is a hot potato. Social Security and deficit reform are two such recent problems. When that occurs, the legislative and executive branch move to a stance of rare cooperation by naming a committee made up of respected experts who offer recommendations for reform.

Generally, the recommendations that emerge because of political gridlock include actions that have been suggested by dominant political figures and groups. Like consultants who borrow a client's watch to give a reading on the time of day, the experts serve an important purpose. They can say and recommend things that would be politically impossible for members of Congress and the President to say, even though many would like to say those things.

Though the time is not yet ripe for such action, a combination of continued command-and-control regulation, slow economic growth, more intense international competition, and rapid technological change could combine to bring a time of reform. Even then, the political limits of environmental control will be encountered.

FINAL THOUGHTS

This book has discussed the political limits of environmental quality regulation. The focus has been on the evolution of the institutions of government designed to regulate environmental use and how people in turn have reacted and responded to institutional change. While telling the environmental saga in terms of political economy, the book has not sought to condemn so much as to explain.

It is sad when scarce human resources are applied to problems in ways that lead to little benefit. In reviewing the chapters of this book, one may conclude that much has been wasted in the nation's effort to improve environmental quality. It is also sad when things as dear as environmental quality are subject to controls and management that provide little in the way of protection. One can easily conclude such is the case in this story.

Conjuring up such conclusions and sentiments has not been the principal purpose of the book. Instead, the purpose of the book is to explain how America's political economy has worked during the years of the environmental saga. Those with strongly held views about environmental regulation and how things might be done better know there are alternatives to the American approach. Records from the past and the actions taken by other societies tell us that things can be done differently.

However, knowing that there are other approaches that might be superior does not allow us to conclude that those solutions can be adopted here. Ours is a political economy, one with political rules that condition outcomes. Change will come when the rules allow it. And the rules allow change only when those who demand change overpower those who demand the status quo. There are political limits to environmental quality regulation.

NOTE

1. Mancur Olson, *The Rise and Decline of Nations* (New Haven: Yale University Press, 1982).

Bibliography

Ackerman, Bruce, and G. Hassler. *Clean Coal/Dirty Air*. New Haven, CT.: Yale University Press, 1981.

"Agency Warns Unit of California Standard on Refinery Emissions." *The Wall Street Journal*. (9 January 1978): 25.

"Air Pollution Control." Information Report No. 20. *Planning Advisory Service*, American Society of Planning Officials (November 1950).

Air/Water Pollution Report. 15, No. 49 (5 December 1977): 481.

Air/Water Pollution Report. 16, No. 3 (16 January 1978): 28.

Air/Water Pollution Report. 16, No. 12 (20 March 1978): 111.

Ames, Bruce N., Renae Magan, and Lois Swirsky Gold. "Ranking Possible Carcinogenic Hazards." *Science* 236, (17 April 1987): 271–80.

Anderson, Eugene R., and Avraham C. Moskowitz. "How Much Does the CGL Pollution Exclusion Really Exclude?" *Risk Management* (August 1984): 29–34.

Anderson, Frederick R., Allen V. Kneese, Phillip D. Reed, et. al. *Environmental Improvement Through Economic Incentives*. Washington: Resources for the Future, 1977.

"Appeals Court Rejects EPA NSPS (New Source Performance Standards) Stationary Source Definition." *Environment Reporter* (10 February 1978): 1569–73.

"Appeals Court Rejects EPA NSPS Stationary Source Definition." *Environment Reporter*, 8, No. 40: 1500.

Ayers, Richard E. "Enforcement of Air Pollution Controls on Stationary Sources Under the Clean Air Amendments of 1970." *Ecology Law Quarterly*, 4, No. 3 (1975): 441–78.

Barnett, Harold C. "The Allocation of Superfund, 1981–1983." *Land Economics*, 61, No. 3 (August 1985): 255–62.

Baumol, William J., and Wallace E. Oates. *Economics, Environmental Policy, and the Quality of Life*. Englewood Cliffs, New Jersey: Prentice Hall, Inc., 1979.

Becker, Gary S. "A Theory of Competition Among Pressure Groups for Political Influence." *The Quarterly Journal of Economics*, 118, No. 3 (August 1983): 371–99.

Bennett, James T., and Thomas J. Dilorenzo. *Destroying Democracy: How Government Funds Partisan Politics*. Washington: Cato Institute, 1985.

Bhansali, Anand, Charles Diamond, and Bruce Yandle. "Sewers as Subsidies." Center for Policy Studies, Clemson University, Clemson, S.C., 1986.

Bonine, John E. "The Evaluation of 'Technology Forcing' in the Clean Air Act." *Environment Reporter Monograph, No. 21*, 6, No. 13 (25 July 1975): 1–30.

Breyer, Stephen. *Regulation and its Reform*. Cambridge: Harvard University Press, 1982.

Broyhill Forum. Appalachian State University, Boone, North Carolina, 11 November 1988.

"The 'Bubble Concept': Industry Chance to Innovate Best-Buy Air Pollution Control." *Congressional Action*. Washington: Chamber of Commerce of the U.S., 23, No. 3, 14 September 1979.

Buchanan, James M. "Rent Seeking and Profit Seeking." In *Toward a Theory of the Rent Seeking Society*, Edited by J.M. Buchanan, R.D. Tollison, and Gordon Tullock. College Station: Texas A&M Press, 1980.

Budget of the United States Government. Washington: Office of Management and Budget, various years.

Calendar of the Patent Rolls. 35 Edward 1, A.D. 1301–7, Leichtenstein: Kraus Reprint (1971): 549.

"California Standard Unit Is Told to Close New Refinery by Pollution Control Panel." *Wall Street Journal*, 25 November 1978.

Christensen, Gregory B., and Robert H. Haveman. "The Reagan Administration's Regulatory Relief: A Mid-Term Assessment." In *The Reagan Regulatory Strategy: An Assessment*, edited by George C. Eads and Michael Fix. Washington: Urban Institute Press (1984): 49–80.

Clark, Timothy B. "New Approaches to Regulatory Reform—Letting the Market Do the Job." *National Journal* (11 August 1979): 1316–22.

Cleary, Edward J. *The Oransco Story*. Resources for the Future, Baltimore: The Johns Hopkins Press, 1967.

The Conservation Foundation. *State of the Environment 1982*. Washington: The Conservation Foundation, 1982.

————. *State of the Environment: An Assessment at Mid-Decade*. Washington: The Conservation Foundation, 1984.

————. *State of the Environment: A View Toward the Nineties*. Washington: The Conservation Foundation, 1987.

Council on Environmental Quality. *Environmental Quality*. Second annual report of the Council on Environmental Quality, Washington: Government Printing Office, August 1971.

————. *Environmental Quality, 1985*. Washington: Council on Environmental Quality, 1988.

Cowan, Thomas A. "Air Pollution Control in New Jersey." *Rutgers Law Review*, 9 (1955): 609–33.

Crandall, Robert W. "Pollution Controls and Productivity Growth in Basic Industries." In *Productivity Measurement in Regulated Industries*, edited by Thomas B. Cowing and Rodney E. Stevenson. New York: Academic Press, 1981.

————. *Controlling Industrial Pollution: The Economics and Politics of Clean Air*. Washington: The Brookings Institution, 1983.

————. *Regulating the Automobile*. Washington: The Brookings Institution, 1986.

"Current Developments." *Environment Reporter* (25 March 1988): 25.

Denison, Edward F. "Explanations of Declining Productivity Growth." *Survey of Current Business* (August 1979): 1–24.

Dobrin, Saxe. Manufacturing Chemists Association meeting, Washington, D.C., 27–28 February 1979.

Downey, George T. *The Significance of Government Policies and Attitudes in Water Pollution Control: A Case Study of the Merrimack River Valley*. Diss. Clark University. Ann Arbor, Michigan: University Microfilms, 1969.

Downing, Paul B. *Environmental Economics and Policy*. Boston: Little, Brown and Company, 1984.

Economic Report of the President, 1971. Washington: Government Printing Office, 1971.

Economic Report of the President, 1978. Washington: Government Printing Office, January 1978.

Environmental Defense Fund. "Petition for the Initiation of Rulemaking Proceedings to Insure Maintenance of the National

Ambient Air Quality Standards and the Prevention of Significant Deterioration Increments in the Ohio River Valley." Presented before the U.S. Environmental Protection Agency, Washington, D.C., 17 July 1978.

Environmental Law Handbook, 8th ed. Rockville, Maryland: Government Institute, Inc., 1985.

"Flammability Rule Argued." *Chemical Engineering News* (9 April 1971): 9.

Florio, James J. "Congress as Reluctant Regulators: Hazardous Waste Policy in the 1980s." *Yale Journal on Regulation*, 3, No. 2 (Spring 1986): 351–82.

Freeman, A. Myrick, and Robert H. Haveman. "Clean Rhetoric and Dirty Water." In *Pollution, Resources, and the Environment*, edited by Alain C. Enthoven and A. Myrick Freeman. New York: W.W. Norton and Company, Inc., 1973.

Fromson, Jeffrey. "A History of Federal Air Pollution Control." *Environmental Law Review—1970*, edited by H. Floyd Sherrod, Jr. Albany, N.Y.: Sage Hill Publishers, Inc., 1970.

Gray, Wayne B. "The Impact of OSHA and EPA Regulation on Productivity." Working Paper No. 1405, National Bureau of Economic Research, Inc., July 1984.

Hahn, Robert W. "Economic Prescriptions for Environmental Problems: Not Exactly What the Doctor Ordered." *Journal of Economic Perspectives*, forthcoming.

Hines, Lawrence D. *Environmental Issues: Population, Pollution, Economics*. New York: W.W. Norton and Company, 1973.

Huber, Peter. "The Environmental Liability Dilemma." *CPCU Journal* (December 1987): 206–16.

————. "Environmental Hazards and Liability Law." In *Liability Perspectives and Policy*, edited by Robert E. Litan and Clifford Winston. Washington: The Brookings Institution (1988): 128–54.

Ingram, Helen M., and Dean E. Mann. "Preserving the Clean Water Act: The Appearance of Environmental Victory." In *Environmental Policy in the 1980s: Reagan's New Agenda*, edited by Norman J. Vig and Michael E. Kraft. Washington: Congressional Quarterly Press, 1984.

Irwin, William A., and Richard A. Liroff. *Economic Disincentives for Pollution Control: Legal, Political, and Administrative Dimensions*. EPA-600/5–74–026, Washington: U.S. Environmental Protection Agency, 1974.

Juergensmeyer, Julian C. "Control of Air Pollution Through the Assertion of Private Rights." *Duke Law Journal* (1967): 1126–44.

Katzman, Martin T. *Chemical Catastrophes: Regulating Environmental Risk Through Pollution Insurance.* Homewood, Ill.: Richard D. Irwin, Inc., 1985.

Kennedy, Harold W. "The Legal Aspects of Air Pollution Control with Particular Reference to the County of Los Angeles." *Southern California Law Review,* 27 (1954): 373–414.

Kennedy, Harold W., and Andrew C. Porter. "Air Pollution: Its Control and Abatement." *Vanderbilt Law Review,* 8 (1985): 854–77.

Kittelman, T.A., and R.B. Akell. "The Cost of Controlling Organic Hydrocarbons." *Chemical Engineering Progress* (April 1978): 87–91.

Kneese, Allen V., and Charles L. Schultze. *Pollution, Prices, and Public Policy.* Washington: The Brookings Institution, 1975.

Kneuper, Robert A. "The Political Economy of Mandatory Passive Restraints: An Investigation of Auto Safety Regulation." Thesis. Department of Economics, Clemson University, 1987.

Krier, James E. *Environmental Law and Policy.* Indianapolis: The Bobbs-Merrill Company, Inc., 1971.

Landau, Jack L. "Who Owns the Air? The Emission Offset Concept and Its Implications." *Environmental Law,* 9, No. 3 (Spring 1979).

Lave, Lester B., and Gilbert S. Omenn. *Cleaning the Air: Reforming the Clean Air Act.* Washington: The Brookings Institution, 1981.

Lieber, Harvey. *Federalism and Clean Water.* Lexington, Mass.: Lexington Books, 1975.

Lipkin, Richard. "Risky Business of Assessing Danger." *Insight* (23 May 1988): 8–13.

MacAvoy, Paul W. *The Regulated Industries and the Economy.* New York: W.W. Norton and Company, 1979.

Maloney, M.T., and Bruce Yandle. "*Building Markets for Tradable Pollution Rights.*" In *Water Rights,* edited by Terry L. Anderson. San Francisco: Pacific Institute for Public Policy Research, 1983.

————. "Estimation of the Cost of Air Pollution Control Regulation." *Journal of Environmental Economics and Management,* 11 (1984): 244–63.

Maloney, Michael T., and Gordon L. Brady. "Capital Turnover and Marketable Pollution Permits." *Journal of Law and Economics,* 31, No. 1 (April 1988): 203–26.

Maloney, Michael T., and Robert E. McCormick. "A Positive Theory of Environmental Quality Regulation." *Journal of Law and Economics*, 25, No. 1 (1982): 99–124.

Marcus, Alfred. "Environmental Protection Agency." In *The Politics of Regulation*, edited by James Q. Wilson. New York: Basic Books (1980): 267–303.

Martin, Douglas. "Curb on Construction Where Air Is Dirty Rankles Businessmen." *The Wall Street Journal* (4 May 1977): 1, 32.

Martin, Robert, and Bruce Yandle. "State Lotteries as Duopoly Transfer Mechanisms." Unpublished manuscript, Department of Economics, Clemson University, 1988.

McChesney, Fred S. "Rent Extraction and Rent Creation in the Economic Theory of Regulation." *The Journal of Legal Studies*, 16 (1987): 101–17.

McNeil, Douglas W., Andrew W. Foshee, and Clark R. Burbee. "Superfund Taxes and Expenditures: Regional Redistribution." *Review of Regional Studies*, 18, No. 1 (Winter 1988): 4–9.

Melnick, R. Shep. *Regulation and the Courts: The Case of the Clean Air Act*. Washington: The Brookings Institution, 1983.

Mill, John Stewart. *Principles of Political Economy*. London: Lambe Publishing, 1862 Edition.

Munn v. Illinois (1877).

Norrell, Todd, and Alexander W. Bell. "Air Pollution Control in Texas." In *Environmental Law Review—1970*, edited by H. Floyd Sherrod. Albany, N.Y.: Sage Hill Publishers, Inc., 1970.

Northsworthy, J.R., Michael J. Harper, and Kent Knuze. "The Slowdown in Productivity Growth: Analysis of Some Contributing Factors." *Brookings Papers on Economic Activity, 1979*, No. 2: 387–421.

Nulty, Peter. "A Brave Experiment in Pollution Control." *Fortune* (12 February 1979): 120–23.

Olson, Mancur. *The Rise and Decline of Nations*. New Haven: Yale University Press, 1982.

Palomba Jr., Joseph. "Air Pollution Control." *The Annals*, 444 (July 1979): 68–69.

Pashigian, B. Peter. "The Effects of Environmental Regulation on Optimal Plant Size and Factor Shares." *Journal of Law and Economics*, 27 (April 1984): 1–28.

———. "Environmental Regulation: Whose Interests Are Being Protected?" *Economic Inquiry*, 23 (October 1985): 551–84.

Peltzman, Sam. "The Effects of Automobile Safety Regulation." *Journal of Political Economy*, 83 (August–December 1975): 677–725.

————. "Toward a More General Theory of Regulation." *Journal of Law and Economics*, 19 (August 1976): 211–40.

Pirsig, Robert. *Zen and the Art of Motorcycle Maintenance*. Toronto: Bantam Books, 1974.

Pollack, Lawrence W. "Legal Boundaries of Air Pollution Control—State and Local Legislative Purpose and Techniques." In *Air Pollution Control*, edited by Clark C. Havinghurst. New York: Oceana Publications, Inc., 1969.

Portney, Paul R. "Reforming Environmental Regulation: Three Modest Proposals." *Issues in Science and Technology*, 4, No. 2 (Winter 1988): 74–81.

Posner, Richard A. "Theories of Economic Regulation." *Bell Journal*, 5 (Autumn 1974): 335–58.

Price, Jamie, and Bruce Yandle. "Labor Markets and Sunday Closing Laws." *Journal of Labor Research*, 8 (Fall 1987): 407–13.

Quarles, John R. "To Grow or Not To Grow—That Is Not the Question." Fifth Annual International Pollution Engineering Congress, Anaheim, California, 10 November 1976.

Quinn, Robert, and Bruce Yandle. "Expenditures on Air Pollution Control Under Federal Regulation." *Review of Regional Studies*, 16, No. 3 (Fall 1986).

Rea, Raymond A. "Hazardous Waste Pollution: The Need For a Different Statutory Approach." *Environmental Law*, 12 (1982): 443–67.

Reinwand, Jerry. "Study of the Evolution of Significant Deterioration." *Environment Reporter* (10 February 1978): 1569–73.

Rich, Bradford W. "Environmental Litigation and the Insurance Dilemma." *Risk Management* (December 1985): 34–41.

Scherer, F.M. "Inter-industry Technology Flows and Productivity Growth." *Review of Economics and Statistics*, 64, No. 4 (1982): 627–34.

Shuford, Gordon, and Bruce Yandle. "Consumer Protection, Private Interest Effects, and Government Liability: The Tris Episode." Unpublished manuscript, Department of Economics, Clemson University, 1988.

Shuman, F.E. "Pittsburgh—'Smokeless City.'" *National Municipal Review*, 39 (November 1950): 489–93.

Smith, Fred L. "Superfund: A Hazardous Waste of Taxpayer Money." *Human Events* (2 August 1986): 662–71.

"Smog—Can Legislation Clear the Air." *Stanford Law Review*, 1 (April 1949): 452–62.

Sowell, Thomas. *A Conflict of Visions*. New York: William Morrow and Company, 1987.

State of the Environment: An Assessment at Mid-Decade. Washington: The Conservation Foundation, 1984.

Stein, Murray. "Problems and Programs in Water Pollution." *Natural Resources Journal*, 2, No. 3 (December 1962): 395–96.

Stern, Arthur C. "Prevention of Significant Deterioration." *Journal of the Air Pollution Control Association*, 27, No. 5 (May 1977), 440–53.

Stigler, George J. "The Theory of Economic Regulation." *Bell Journal* (Spring 1971), 3–21.

"Superfund: A Game of Chance." *Natural Resources and Environment*, 1, No. 3 (Fall 1985), symposium issue.

Survey and Investigations Staff. "A Report to the Committee on Appropriations, U.S. House of Representatives, on the Status of the Environmental Protection Agency's Superfund Program." (March 1988): 9.

Tarr, Joel A. "Urban Pollution—Many Years Ago." *American Heritage*, 22 (October 1971).

Tietenberg, Tom. *Emissions Trading: An Exercise in Reforming Pollution Policy*. Washington: Resources for the Future, 1985.

———. *Environmental and Natural Resource Economics*. Glenville, Ill.: Scott, Foresman and Company, 1988.

Tullock, Gordon. "The Welfare Costs of Tariffs, Monopolies, and Theft." *Western Economic Journal*, 5 (June 1967): 224–32.

U.S. Congress, Committee on Government Operations, 91st Congress, 2nd Session, "Qui Tam Actions and the 1899 Refuse Act: Citizens Lawsuits Against Polluters of the Nation's Waterways," 1970.

U.S. Department of Commerce. *Regulatory Reform Seminar*. (October 1978): A66–A70.

U.S. Department of Energy. *United States Energy Policy, 1980–1988*. Washington: U.S. Department of Energy (October 1988): 152.

U.S. Environmental Protection Agency. "Emission Offset Interpretative Ruling." *Federal Register*, 44, No. 11 (16 January 1979).

———. "Air Pollution Control: Recommendations for Alternative Emission Reduction Options Within State Implementation Plans." *Federal Register*, 44, No. 13 (18 January 1979).

———. *The Cost of Clean Air and Water Report to Congress*, 1984, Executive Summary, Washington: U.S. Environmental Protection Agency (May 1984).

———. "Unfinished Business: A Comparative Assessment of Environmental Problems: Overview Report." Washington: U.S. Environmental Protection Agency (February 1987).

U.S. General Accounting Office. *Improvements Needed in Controlling Major Air Pollution Sources.* Washington: General Accounting Office, 1978.

———. "Hazardous Waste: Issues Surrounding Insurance Availability." GAP/RCED-88-2, Washington: U.S. General Accounting Office (October 1987).

Warren, Melinda, and Kenneth Chilton. *1989 Federal Regulatory Budgets and Staffing: Effects of the Reagan Presidency.* St. Louis: Center for the Study of American Business, Washington University, April 1988.

"Water Pollution, Pesticide Residues, and Cancer." *Water,* 27, No. 2 (Summer 1986): 23–4.

Weiss, Leonard W., and Allyn D. Strickland. *Regulation: A Case Approach.* 2nd ed. New York: MacGraw-Hill Book Company, 1982.

Wildavsky, Aaron. *Searching for Safety.* Bowling Green, Ohio: Social Philosophy and Policy Center, 1988.

Yandle, Bruce. "The Emerging Market in Air Pollution Rights." *Regulation* (July/August 1978): 21–29.

———. "Buying and Selling for Cleaner Air?" *Business* (March/April 1979, 29, No. 2: 33–36.

———. "Economic Agents and the Level of Pollution Control." *Public Choice,* 40, No. 1 (1983).

———. "Environmental Control and Regional Growth." *Growth and Change,* 15, No. 3 (July 1984): 39–42.

———. "A Public Choice Interpretation of Environmental User Charges and Superfund." *CATO Journal,* forthcoming.

———. "Sulfur Dioxide: State Versus Federal Control." *The Journal of Energy and Development,* 10, No. 1 (Autumn 1984): 63–69.

———. "Bootleggers and Baptists in the Market for Regulation." In *The Political Economy of Government Regulation,* edited by Jason F. Shogren. Norwell, Mass.: Kluwer Academic Publishers, forthcoming.

Yannacone Jr., Victor J., and Bernard Cohen. *Environmental Rights and Remedies,* Vol. 1, Rochester, N.Y.: The Lawyers Cooperate Publishing Company, 1972.

Zuesse, Eric. "Love Canal: The Truth Seeps Out." *Reason* (February 1981): 17–33.

Index

About the Author

BRUCE YANDLE is Alumni Professor of Economics at Clemson University. He coedited *Politicians, Bureaucracy and the Public Interest, Public Choice: An Inside View of the F.T.C.*, *The Strategic Use of Regulation for Anticompetitive Purposes,* and *Benefit-Cost Analyses of Social Regulation.* Yandle wrote *Labor and Property Rights in California Agriculture: An Economic Analysis of the CALRA, Managing Personal Finance,* and *Environmental Use and the Market.* In addition, he has written numerous articles published in *Public Choice, Journal of Environmental Economics and Management,* and *Quarterly Review of Economics and Business,* among other publications.